WE'RE ALL A MESS, IT'S OK

Amy
Lyle

Cover design and photography by
Andrea Ferenchik of Andrea Linn Photography

© 2018 Amy Lyle

For permissions contact: AmyLyle.com

ISBN 978-0-9989684-1-4

THIS BOOK IS DEDICATED TO THE CONTRIBUTORS WHO SHARED THEIR FAILURES, SET-BACKS AND EMBARRASSING MOMENTS WITH THE HOPES THAT THEIR STORIES WILL GIVE THE WEARY SOME RELIEF. YOU ARE A RARE FIND, TO REVEAL THE TRUTH, UNFILTERED AND AUTHENTIC. THANK YOU FOR INSPIRING SO MANY STORIES.

AND . . . TO PETER, WHO LOVES ME IN SPITE OF ME.

Many stories in this book are true.

But some are lies.

Kudos for The Book of Failures

The Amy Binegar-Kimmes-Lyle Book of Failures has been a bestseller on Amazon since it's release. In October of 2018, it reached number one on Amazon in *"Humor Essays"*, *"Humor & Entertainment: Parenting & Families"* as well as *"Humor & Entertainment: Step-parenting & Blended Families"*.

Reviews

"The funniest, wittiest, and most-relatable book a girl could read."

~ A. Evers
   Blue Line Scripture

"If you have ever been married, divorced, had a relationship where he/she was not that into you, been a student, s*** your pants, had a crazy-awesome friend, or have kids in your life, you'll find something relatable in this book.

~ Jessica Van Derven
   Writer, WisconsinTrophyWife.com

"This book will make you feel, as a woman and as a mother, that you suck less."

~Angie Stati

Contents

SWIPE LEFT FOR NO-DATING FAILS

I make mistakes,
I'll be the second to admit it.
~ Jean Kerr

My First Date and a Sluggish Toilet

When I was sixteen, Jeff Jordon, asked me out on a date. He had just recently come off full-on orthodontics headgear at the beginning of the school year and people had not yet caught on to his smokin' hotness. My mother dropped me off at his house (the nicest house in our town) to have dinner. After drilling his parents for ten minutes about the "activities" allowed in their home, she made SEVERAL points about how the parents were responsible for not allowing me to be in any situations that would jeopardize my chaste state as one day I would be taking sanctioned marriage vows. Oddly, she agreed to let his parents drive me home.

We sat down for dinner at their large mahogany dinning room table that would easily seat sixteen. Jeff and I sat on one side and his parents on the other. Mrs. Jordon asked me at least ten times if I was enjoying my dinner, which I wasn't because she had put the top four foods that I hated, broccoli, beans, onions and mayonnaise, all into one salad. I could hear my mother's voice telling me I would be rude not to eat what was offered so I choked it down in between bites of a cheesy chicken casserole.

After dinner, we watched a movie in the living room. Jeff and I sat in Queen Anne chairs flanked on each side of a Duncan Phyfe sofa, where his parents were sitting. After the movie, Mr. Jordon announced that it was getting late, so he'd drive me back. His wife and Jeff said they would ride with us, but as we were headed out, I excused myself to "wash my hands" in the powder room. Although broccoli, beans, and onions were on my all-time least favorite food list, they must have topped the "foods that give you gas" list, as I thought I was going to explode.

I thought they would head outside, but they all waited in the fancy foyer. I could hear Mr. Jordan pacing on the harlequin tiles that ran from the foyer, through the long hall, to the bathroom. I ran the water and kept flushing the toilet to cover my loud gas. Finally, I pulled up my pants and realized the water was rising and would overflow.

Jeff knocked on the door and asked if I was alright. The poo was edging to the top of the bowl and there was not a trash can or a window to throw the floater into.

"There's water running into the foyer!" exclaimed Mr. Jordon. "Open the door!"

Desperate and in a panic, I grabbed the poo and threw it into my purse. Later, after the towels were taken to the washing machine and the water was turned off to the toilet, the Jordon's tried to limit my embarrassment by saying the home was old and they were used to frequent overflows. With the mess cleaned up, we all braved the freezing night to get into their car.

You may wonder, how long does it take a fresh poo to stink up a car? The answer is … immediately. I kept rolling down the window, saying I was hot, even though the temperature was below freezing outside. That was my first and last date with Jeff Jordon.

~ Kim Banta, Actress

We All Do Not Scream for Ice Cream

Despite my parents' and friends' disapproval, I started dating Scott, an intern from work who was seven years my junior who made minimum wage and lived with his parents. I defended the super-hot, just-out-of-college soccer player, stating that one of the first questions he had asked me at work was about the performance of our 401(k) plan. In my eyes, he was more mature than many of the men I knew and, more importantly, far-removed from the thirty-five-year-old feckless flunky that I had married and divorced a few years ago.

Scott's parents were out of town and my roommate's parents were visiting (and staying at our apartment), so it was the perfect opportunity to have a romantic weekend together. When I arrived at his place, midday, we made love for the first time. In my post-sex euphoria, I was thinking that the amateur analyst was quite qualified in the bedroom.

I lit a cigarette and had not even exhaled when we heard the jingle of the ice-cream truck. Scott jumped out of bed and started opening all his drawers, saying, "I need quarters. The ice-cream truck! I need quarters!" He hopped out the door, putting on his pants as he went, and ran outside.

When he came back in and saw me still naked in his bed, looking around his room decorated with trophies and banners going back to his elementary school days, he realized how ridiculous it had been for him to practically jump off me to get ice cream.

I expected him to be embarrassed, but he was proud. He had two caramel sundae cones in his hands. He sat on the bed, kissed me, and said, "I got this for you."

We were married within the year.
    ~ Marie Acuri

Saying "I'm Sorry" Will Not Fix This Situation

I turned the best date I ever had into the worst date when I aggressively jumped on my partner, trying to straddle him. He screamed, "You broke my penis!" I didn't believe him, but the emergency room nurse informed me that the condition is called a penile fracture and it happens when an erect penis sustains brunt force. After I took him home from the ER, we never spoke again as it was too awkward. I couldn't text him and ask, "So, how's your penis?"
    ~ Ashley P.

Oh, Nikki!

When I was in high school, I started dating a girl named Nikki shortly after she had a dramatic breakup with her meathead jock boyfriend, Chuck. Everyone knew Chuck. He wore only Buffalo Bills jerseys, took steroids to enhance his hulking physique, and had a reputation for being controlling and rough with his girlfriends.

I was at lunch with a group of friends when Chuck approached me, his hands out to strangle me. He got a firm grip on my neck, but I put both my arms up the middle and broke loose. We grappled on the cafeteria floor for a few minutes before teachers broke us up and forced us to shake hands. I thought the issue was resolved.

That Friday at the football game, I was facing the field when, from behind me, I heard, "Nikki's my woman!" I turned to see Chuck, ready to rumble.

To make matters worse, Chuck's elderly mother was also with him, holding one of her high-heeled shoes like a billy club, screaming, "You don't mess with my boy!"

It was a surreal moment where I thought I would have to fight Chuck and his mother. My friend Scott Condo got a sleeper hold on Chuck, while I blocked Chuck's mom's shoe shots until we were all escorted out of the stadium.

Chuck and I were both suspended from school for fighting but the real battle was for Nikki. Chuck said, "What about my girl?" I threw my hands in the air in disbelief, "She doesn't want you, she wants me." It was at that point that

Nikki appeared. "Nikki, tell Chuck it's over and you've moved on," I suggested to settle the score once and for all. Nikki turned to Chuck and said "I love you Chuck!", and she walked off with him and his mother.

~ Scott Specker

Hello Father

Many years ago, a guy I was dating said he'd call me Saturday morning around eleven to finalize plans for Saturday night. When the phone rang at eleven, I answered, saying, "Hey, Handsome Dan, what's the scoop?" There was a long pause. "Hello?" I said.

"It's Father McCullagh," a low-voice announced. It was the town priest, collecting money for a Catholic charity.

~ R Lynn Barnett,
  Author, *What Patients Want: Anecdotes and Advice*

This Is Awkward

My senior year my parents uprooted our family and moved us from New Jersey to North Carolina. I had been dating the same boy all through high school, but we had never had sex. Faced with being pulled away from all my friends and losing the love of my life, I caved. The night before we moved, we had sex in my parents' unfinished basement under the guise of playing ping-pong. My un-blossoming took approximately 87 seconds.

My mother and I went to North Carolina while my dad

finished up some business with his old company, and I cried the whole way there. She also booked both of us for every medical exam possible—a vision check, a complete physical, a teeth cleaning (plus fluoride), and even gynecological exams—because she said she didn't know how long it would take to get the new insurance coverage.

The OB/GYN was a very handsome guy in his forties. He asked if I was sexually active. I sheepishly shared the story about leaving the love of my life and how we lost our virginity our last night together. He took off his glasses, rubbed his temples, and broke the news that I had sexually transmitted genital warts. My New Jersey love was not as faithful as I had believed. The treatment was cryotherapy, burning the warts off with liquid nitrogen. I was sobbing uncontrollably, thinking about the betrayal, the loss of my innocence, and frankly the humiliation of a handsome doctor concentrating so intently on my vagina. I never told my mother.

I finally adjusted to my new school, joined the musical theatre group, and started visiting colleges and dating my chemistry partner, Seth. After about a month, he invited me to spend the day boating with his family on Lake Mattamuskeet. We drove to the lake and his mom picked us up in a small whaler to take us to their large houseboat that was docked in a cove. We spent the day swimming and lying out on the top deck with his two sisters and his family friends.

Around dinner time, Seth's dad and uncle arrived and we all sat down for dinner. Seth's father, seated across from me, extended his hand and warmly said, "I've heard so much about you. I'm Dr. Hayes."

It took less than two seconds for both of us, awkwardly shaking hands in our swimwear, to recognize one another. He was the physician who had burned off my genital warts.
~ Shirley S.

The Interruption
In between the Mississippi State game and the after-party, a cute guy that I had been partying with invited me back to his house to hang out. He and his roommate lived in a trailer, just off campus.

We were listening to music and making out on his bed when I saw a giant rat. My date ran from the room, returning to hand me a tennis racquet, saying, "If he comes out when I move the dresser, whack him with this." As he lifted the dresser, the rodent ran right toward me. I swung the racquet like a golf club and managed to make contact, dazing the creature. My date threw the rat into a laundry bag, tied it up and threw it in the trash.

He returned the dresser to its original spot and we resumed making out.
~ Shauna Dann

Go West

I had landed a great job in Utah and was moving over the weekend, so a few coworkers threw me a farewell party at the office. One of the other analysts had shared that she had an old college friend, James, that lived in the same area that I was moving to, so she introduced us via email. James told me he would let me get settled, and then if I was up to grabbing coffee, he'd show me around my new city.

Two weeks into my new surroundings, I was excited to receive a message from James about getting together. We hit it off immediately and started spending a lot of time together. James had an older son, John, who lived with him full-time, although he was a little vague about his son's occupation. I understood he was a student who had a part-time social-media job that he worked from home.

As James and I were planning to walk to get ice cream, I invited John to join us. I had asked him several times previously to lunch or dinner, but he had always declined, using food-related excuses, such as allergies to gluten, artificial food dyes or GMO products. I thought this was his polite way of turning us down, as James never insisted that he come. This evening John simply said, "I can't," to my ice cream offer.

I tried to make light of his rejection and said, "Lactose intolerant?"

"No," John said, as he pulled up the leg of his jeans to reveal a real-time GPS ankle-bracelet tracker. "House arrest."

~ L.B.A.

Plot Twist

When I was fifteen, I wanted to seduce my boyfriend, Michael. My ideas about seduction were based on the soap opera *One Life to Live*, which my mother insisted on watching every day. She would tell my father at the dinner table about Marty and Patrick surviving Irish assassins and how everyone in Llanview was plotting to pull Nora and Bo apart as fervently as Christiane Amanpour would report on an infectious-disease outbreak on CNN. Anyway, my goal was to get him to French kiss me.

My parents were taking my brother to his pediatrician for a checkup and would be gone for at least an hour, so I invited Michael over. He arrived on his Schwinn and I lured him into our basement with the promise of necking AND Doritos. I showed Michael into the small rec room that my younger brother used to build his LEGO creations and asked him to sit on the sofa.

Wearing a sheer T-shirt that I tied in the middle like Daisy Duke would have done, I entered the room and dramatically closed the door. As I started my "sexy walk" toward him, I said something to the effect of "Are you ready?" I was running my hands up my body where curves should have been but weren't yet.

When I was within one step of him, I decided I would impress him with a kick. (Michael was a big fan of old Bruce Lee movies.) I hadn't planned or practiced the kick but I jumped really high and threw out a modified Taekwondo roundhouse. I yelled, "Hi-yah!" as I kicked my leg up and then came down, hard, feeling the most excruciating pain. I dropped to the floor, turned my foot over, and saw a tiny LEGO embedded in my arch.

I started a loud screaming/cussing/crying combination that vacillated between "It's in my foot!" and "Mother*****r!"

That's when my parents started banging on the door until it opened and discovered a teenage boy with a full erection hovering over their crying daughter dressed as a soap-opera seductress bleeding on the carpet amongst my brother's Jurassic World Indoraptor Rampage at Lockwood Estate and the Harry Potter Quidditch Match LEGO sets.

After a visit to the emergency room and getting a minor suture, I was grounded for several weeks. I didn't land my first French kiss until the following summer.

    ~ Haleigh Rhea Nesbitt

Arrgh

Two years post-divorce, I reluctantly agreed to sign up for a dating app, having had no success in that arena since my divorce. On the brink of throwing in the towel with online dating due to a medley of disasters (including the discovery that two suitors were married – they used their real names and prominently displayed their wife and family on their Facebook pages – and from another, the surprise arrival of an unsolicited video of his manhood "on the rise"), I received a compelling inquiry that gave me hope.

His name was Nick. He disclosed that he was in his mid-forties, had also been divorced for two years, enjoyed spending time with his kids, and loved documentaries. Nick and I corresponded for over a month before we went on our first date, after a break finally came in our work/kids/travel schedules. We agreed to meet at an Italian restaurant.

When I walked in, I saw him at the bar. As he turned to hug me, he revealed an eyepatch. I launched into telling him how sorry I was and asked how he had injured himself, as he was not wearing an eyepatch in his match.com profile. He put his hand on my shoulder, as if to calm me, and whispered in my ear, "I'm not injured. I just like to be edgy."

We went on two more dates before I called it quits. For date number two he wore a carpal-tunnel wrist wrap, and when I suggested he stop pretending he had injuries, I thought we were on the same page … until he showed up on what ended up being our last date because he had an Aircast boot on his left foot.

I eventually – and accidentally – met someone and fell in love. Bob and I met in the Sam's Soak and Suds commercial washer section. We were both pretreating red-wine stains, he on a white slipcover and me on a duvet. Sometimes it's just when you give up that love shows up.

~ A.D.B.

No Connection

My freshman year at Ohio State I met a super-hot guy in English 101. His roommates were too cheap to buy cable and they didn't have a DVD player, so we were always at my place.

He had shared with me that in high school he had been a superstar wrestler so, as we were watching TV on the sofa, I asked him if he wanted to grapple. We fell to the floor and were rolling around when he thought he had me in a hold I couldn't escape. I was able to (or he let me) get one knee up under him and that was all I needed to swing my other leg around, but I also accidentally caught the cord to the television and ripped it off the table onto his head. He was bleeding profusely. We spent the next few hours in the emergency room.

We dated for a few weeks, but it was awkward. I felt guilty about breaking his head open and he kept apologizing about our smashed Magnavox. I went to the doctor with him for his final check. The doctor cleared him, saying he could resume all physical activity. As we headed back, I asked him if he wanted to hang out and maybe partake in some physical activity.

"Did you get another TV?" he asked.

When I replied, "Not yet", he told me he would just rather go home.
~ Mary S.

Not a Good Surprise
My date and I were walking down the street to our car when a naked, hairy man jumped out of the bushes and flashed us. We then rode around in the back of the police cruiser looking for the streaker until 3:00 a.m.
~ Jaime E

And, We're Done
We got along great until he introduced me to his children. They were feral.
~ Kristin L.

Want to Talk about It?
My worst date ever was when a guy talked about his ex-girlfriend the entire time we were at dinner. When we got into his car and he started to go on again, I said, "You should contact her. It sounds like you have some stuff to work out."

He took action immediately and pulled over into a Krystal

parking lot to call her. He spoke for at least five minutes and then put the phone down in defeat – she had hung up on him. I said I was so sorry because I didn't know what else to say. He scooted over and cried on my shoulder for half an hour. He asked if I wanted to go back to his place, but I declined.

~ Michele Robinson
randominsanity-ifididntlaugh.blogspot.com

Little White Lie

We lived in a large house and next door was a property with the same floor-plan that had been converted to flats. I used to lean out the window because the guy in the next building was so hot. I would watch him get into his convertible MG and drive off with his supermodel-looking girlfriend. He was so beautiful, I would stare at him, mesmerized. Sometimes, his eyes would catch mine and he would smile as I blushed beet-red.

I had bleached my hair blonde, but I couldn't afford to keep up with the maintenance of the roots, so I had a reverse-skunk look going with several inches of black hair abruptly meeting the bleached half. I finally dyed it dark again and pushed it all up into a ponytail. I looked like a totally different person as I leaned out the window that night.

"Hello!" I heard and turned to see my hot neighbor leaning out, looking at me. He continued, "Do you have any milk?"

I checked the refrigerator and ran back. "Yes. Do you have any matches?"

He replied, "Of course."

"I'll bring the milk over," I said, "and you can give me the matches." I went over to his apartment with plans of being naughty.

When he let me in, he said, "There's another girl that lives next door, with the black-and-white striped hair? Why don't you invite her over as well?"

I was mortified and made up a lie on the spot. "Umm, that was a friend that was in town, staying with us for just a few weeks. She went back to Australia."
    ~ Caroline Sherouse,
        Author, *Blow Me Over with a Feather*

Get Out

Three years after my divorce, and a few weeks before my fortieth birthday, I finally created a profile on a popular dating app, at the urging of my family and friends. After about three weeks of messaging Bruce, the 45-year-old engineer, four-years-divorced, no kids and loves dogs "match", we scheduled our first rendezvous. We were meeting in downtown Atlanta at The Fox Theatre to see the renowned Alvin Ailey dancers. The performance was outstanding, and the date was going so well that we headed to a restaurant to have dessert and a drink.

Bruce and I shared a bottle of champagne and then another as we laughed about some of the bizarre profiles and encounters we had experienced as singles. Before leaving the restaurant, we made second-date plans for a comedy show coming up in a few weeks. As we stood to leave, the champagne really hit me, and I became a little dizzy. Bruce helped me to his car. He asked if he should drive me home or if we should go back to his place to sober up and watch an old stand-up special of the comedienne we would be seeing in a few weeks. I opted for the latter.

Bruce lived in Buckhead, a swanky part of Atlanta, in a lovely 1960s house that had been completely remodeled. I drank about a gallon of water as we watched the comedy special and I started to feel a lot better. When Bruce settled me into the guest room, providing me a stack of clean towels, he told me how much he had enjoyed the evening and kissed me very lightly. I hadn't been kissed in years. The whole night had been wonderful, and he was such an honest, nice guy. I returned his gentlemanly kiss by pulling him onto me.

I was blissfully sleeping when Bruce came tearing into the room, scream-whispering, "My parents are home, my parents are home." He was ushering me into a walk-in closet while tossing my shoes, dress and undergarments on top of me. "Shhhh," he said.

I was hopping on one foot, putting my shoe on, when his mother opened the closet door. "BRUCE!" she screamed. "Not ANOTHER one!" She draped my handbag around my head, handed me my other shoe and shuffled me out the door.

I walked down the winding driveway, expecting Bruce to pick me up and drive me back to the theatre to get my car, but he never did.

~ Naomi L.

Too Much

In preparation for my thirtieth high school reunion, I had lost close to twenty pounds, started a spin class, and traded my glasses for contacts. A week before the big event, I got Botox treatments in my forehead, a first for me. The dermatologist recommended I get very little, but I insisted on doing the maximum, for the biggest effect.

Within two days, my face looked like it had melted and then cooled; it was very contorted. I had already paid for the flight and was hoping my face would settle by the time of the event.

It had not. All night at the reunion, people looked at my high school picture on my name tag, then back at me. They would say either, "You look very different," or they would ask if I had been in an accident.

~ Terry A.

IN THE MORNING

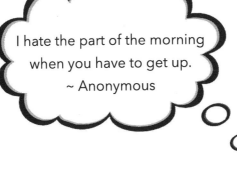

I hate the part of the morning
when you have to get up.
~ Anonymous

Nothing Is Free

I was only introduced to Starbucks a few years ago. I don't get why there are entire stores dedicated to cups of coffee that cost as much as a pound. My daughter and I would go occasionally, and she would treat me to a chai tea latte, which I love. So, as I headed to my twin-granddaughters' graduation party, I was feeling groggy and thought a shot of caffeine would help perk me up.

As I waited in line, I picked up two cute coffee mugs for the graduates and a couple gift cards. I also noticed a few signs promoting a new product, so when I ordered my chai tea latte, I told the cashier I wanted to try their newest product. She kept looking down, as if trying to locate the special of the day, so I said, "I would like to try the free sample of the weefey."

The cashier said, "I'm so sorry. I've just started this week and I'm not familiar with that promotion. We don't really have any free promotions going on right now. Maybe that was a while ago?"

I huffed and pointed out not one, not two, but three different signs in the store advertising the promotion. The cashier's eyebrows went up, but before she could speak, Meg, an old student of mine, stepped out of line. (I had been a teacher for over thirty years and was frequently recognized.)

I said, "Hello, Meg!" and I hugged her.

"Mrs. Hale," Meg replied, "the signs say 'Wi-Fi,' for free Internet access. It's not a drink or a snack."

I looked to the cashier, to all the people standing in line, and then back to Meg. I walked out the door, mortified. I haven't been back to a coffeehouse since.

~ Carole Hale

I Thought It Was the Tacos

I went to work one morning and wondered out loud to a coworker why my pants felt so small. She told me I had them on backwards – and that my name tag was upside down. Then I was counting the hours until 4:00 p.m.

~ S.G.

What a Pitiful Moment

Rushing out the door to make it to an appointment, I quickly spritzed my pits with what I thought was deodorant. It wasn't. It was dry shampoo, which looks just like the deodorant bottle.

~ Becky Dent Robinson

Casual Day

When I was called to present my piece at the board meeting, I pushed back from the boardroom table and realized I was still wearing slippers.

~ B.H.

I am Not Fonda Her

I was minding my own business, waiting in line at the coffee shop, when the guy in front of me turned around, paused, and said, "You look just like that actress Bridget Fonda."

I smiled and replied, "Thanks! I know who she is. I've seen a couple of her movies."

As he turned toward the cashier, he looked annoyed and grumbled, "I never thought she was attractive."

~ A.B.L.

Right Place, Wrong Time

I was so excited to have secured an interview with a radio station in town. I lived in the suburbs, thirty miles away, but the commute took over an hour with the bumper-to-bumper traffic. I ran up the steps to the second floor and asked for the manager. "He's not in yet," the receptionist said flatly. I was grateful that I had beat him to the office. I sat in the lobby and pulled up the job description on my phone, getting as prepared as I could for the meeting. After an hour, I got slightly indignant with the receptionist, telling her about my commute, and asking where Robert the host was that I was meeting with. She asked for my name, looked in the computer and smirked. "Robert is the host of the late show. Your interview is not until 8:00 pm."

~ John H.

WE SHOULD HAVE STAYED HOME
- TRAVEL DISASTERS

Whoever is in charge of making sure
I don't do stupid shit is fired.
~ Anonymous

Why, Thank You

My friend Carol and I had been friends for close to forty years when we had planned a trip to South Florida to escape the winter blahs in Atlanta. Once we were settled in the hotel, we headed off to a recommended beach for a hike, climbing down a rocky incline to enjoy the sunshine and beautiful, clear water.

It was about midday when a military helicopter passed us and we could have sworn we heard them whistling. We were thrilled, as we were both closer to fifty than forty. When the helicopter went by again, this time we could see a service guy looking down and shouting, "Whoo, ladies, looking great!" As we lay on our towels, we gave them a salute and giggled.

Carol suggested we flash the servicemen; after all, they risked their lives for us every day. We agreed that Carol would flash them her boobs and I would moon them. Within the hour, we heard the helicopter approaching and we sprang into action. Carol ripped off her tankini top and I pulled down my pants. As the men flew by, they waved and appeared to be screaming at us. It made our day. We kept teasing one another that we still had "it" if young, handsome Navy pilots were whooping it up for us.

At sunset, we packed all our things and headed up the rocks. To our surprise, there were over fifty COLLEGE-aged, bikini-clad, young ladies hanging out at the top. We allowed ourselves to be disappointed for a few minutes, knowing the servicemen were cheering for them and not us, but the story is so funny, we tell it every chance we get.

~ Anonymous

Something's Touching Me

My best friend and I were ecstatic to be going to the US Open. It was an extremely hot day and we had consumed a case of water, which meant we had to hustle to the porta-potty in between matches. Long before we reached it, we could smell the restroom.

One guest passed us and advised, "Do not touch anything in there."

When it was my turn, I took this advice to heart and chose the hover technique, perfected during my years spent peeing in college bar bathrooms. I undid my pants and squatted, which really burned my thighs as I didn't even touch the walls to balance myself. Within seconds, I felt something warm and wet splashing on my feet but I couldn't stop peeing midstream.

When I finished, I looked for a water leak and didn't see anything. It was only when I stood up to zip my pants that I realized that, because of my commitment to touch nothing and in my haste to pee, I had peed on the lid, creating a splash.

~ Andrea F.

When I returned to my car after a weeklong business trip I was greeted by one million ants. I threw a pile of clothes on my seat and headed to the first car wash to vacuum them out. They were living off an opened Tic-Tac container that had spilled in my glove box. During the hour and a half drive home, I literally had ants in my pants.

~ Leslie

She May Be Dead, We're Not Sure

Our parents got a sitter from the hotel, so they could enjoy an evening out in Toronto. The service sent us a ninety-year-old lady named Middie who fell asleep in the chair while my cousins and I jumped back and forth from bed to bed so aggressively we broke a leg on one of the beds. When our parents came back and called for maintenance to come and repair it (at a cost of $200), the sitter continued to sleep. My parents did not want to jostle her, for fear she'd have a heart attack, so we all just sat in our beds, watching TV, and Middie, until she finally woke up.

~ Bleu C.

Just a Little off the Top

On a recent trip back to my hometown for a business meeting, I took a few extra days to visit my parents and catch up with old friends. I had moved to Knoxville, gotten married and had a real job. To the townies, I was quite a big deal.

After I unpacked my bags, I went to the bathroom to

freshen up before going out. When I bent down to reapply my lipstick using my mom's 10x light-up mirror on the counter, I was confronted with the truth that no one in their twenties wants to admit: I did a fair job of keeping my eyebrows from growing together but had never thought twice about old-lady lip hairs.

I hastily applied some of Mom's wax with the small, ice-cream-social wooden-spoon-style applicator, skipping the step about warming it first because I was in a hurry. I counted to three and ripped it off … and blood went everywhere. I had ripped off my skin. I lied to my coworkers and to my friends, telling them that I had been partying so hard, drinking backdrafts (a drink you ignite), that I had burned the skin from my top lip to the base of my nose. I don't think any of them fell for it.
~ Jessica Van Derven
Writer, WisconsinTrophyWife.com

I Am Not Prepared

I convinced my husband and son that I could handle the rigor and what was required of Boy Scout camp. They reluctantly agreed that I could go. My husband told me to pack only the bare essentials and to, "hydrate, hydrate, hydrate." I must have had six bottles of water on the way to the site. As we were preparing to take off for a five-mile hike, the bathroom facilities were occupied, so I took the opportunity to tell my son that I was going old-school, in the woods, like a real camper. I swatted behind a tree and proceeded to accidentally pee into my boots. I was miserable during the hike, as I had only brought one pair of boots.

~ Jenna Kovacik Turner

Forget the Whole Thing

For a family vacation, I had originally planned to fly from LAX to D.C. and then drive down with family to a condo in Myrtle Beach, South Carolina. For the return trip, I'd catch a ride to Raleigh/Durham and fly from there to LAX.

I had spaced-out completely and let my ride leave me at the Myrtle Beach airport.

The clerk told me I could get a flight to Raleigh/Durham, but it would cost me $800. I tried to rent a car and drive to Raleigh/Durham, but National Car Rental was expecting their new fleet, so they had shipped all their old cars away. Unfortunately, the new fleet had not shown up, and they had no cars.

A bus trip would take eighteen hours, so I thought, "Maybe a taxi?" But all the taxis were taken up by elderly golfers … except for one, owned and driven by "Skink," who agreed to drive me to Raleigh/Durham for $350. I had to go to three different ATMs before I could get the cash together, but we finally set off for Raleigh/Durham during a heavy rain in Skink's ancient Chevrolet, which had a hole in the floor on the passenger side.

Skink brought along a bottle of peach schnapps, which he sipped from now and again as he discussed religion and I listened, inserting comments like, "Oh ... is that right ... I never knew that ... gosh ... really ... snake-handling sounds dangerous," and so on.

I arrived at the Holiday Inn late at night, begged for food from a just-closed kitchen, got up the next day, went to the airport, paid all kinds of penalties and all the taxes, and finally flew home. I wish I could say that this was my worst vacation ever, but it wasn't.

~ Dana Huse
Author, *Coyote Truck Maintenance*

Total Collapse

When our kids were little, my husband, Jim, and I took them to the Chattanooga Aquarium. We did not have a double stroller but knowing it would be helpful for a day like this, we borrowed my older sister's. She asked us if we wanted a lesson on setting it up and breaking it down and we laughed at her, saying that we thought we could figure out a baby stroller.

Once we arrived, we took the kids and all the baby paraphernalia out of the car, loaded it into the stroller, and headed to the ticket counter. When we got to the first crosswalk, we paused for the signal to turn green. When it did, Jim quickly pushed the stroller off the curb and into the street. As the stroller went off the curb, it collapsed, and because Jim was pushing full force behind it, he fell forward onto it. The stroller folded up like a taco with two girls inside. The other pedestrians' facial expressions ranged from shock and concern to suppressed laughter at the pileup.

Jim sprung back up faster than he fell and yanked the stroller handles up. Jim and I were looking at the girls - who were fine - and the stroller. What had we done wrong? As we continued to ponder it, another mom pushing the exact model stopped beside us, ever so casually, and without a word, she motioned to the stroller lock, nodded, and moved on. We never admitted our crash to my sister.
~ Jim and Susan Holloway

Is This Our Stop?

My best friend and I used to teach elementary school together, and during one particularly rough year, we planned a spring break trip to Puerto Vallarta, Mexico. We made up fake stories about who we were and why we were there and proceeded to drink our way through the week.

One day when we were out exploring, we saw a Walmart and decided to check it out and see if a Mexican Walmart was the same as the American version. We loaded up on Mexican candy and went back to the bus stop to head back to the hotel. Once we got on the bus and started riding around, we enjoyed the sights, sounds, and smells of our adventure, we noticed we were getting farther away from the tourist areas.

Unsure what to do and unable to speak enough Spanish to do any more than ask for beer or the bathroom, we just kept riding and figured eventually we'd get back to where we started. We rode, and rode, and rode. We saw shopping areas and many residential areas, and eventually we were the last two people on the bus. The bus driver said something to us, and we just smiled and nodded and explained in English where we were trying to go. He shrugged, and we kept riding - straight out of town.

We started to panic, wondering if we'd be sexually violated before we were murdered or after, and decided that, if given a choice, we'd prefer after. We rode all the way to a beach, where the driver stopped, turned off the bus, and motioned that we had to leave before exiting himself. Once we were all off the bus, he pointed down the beach and then joined a group of people who were drinking and having a cookout. We started walking and could hear everyone laugh as we left.

We walked and walked in the direction he had pointed, and eventually, after not drinking or eating all day long and walking on the scalding hot sand, we finally saw the giant orange wall of our hotel in the distance. As soon as we were within the gates, we were so relieved to still be alive - and, of course, we were very, very thirsty.

~ Liz Reyes

Emergency Room Spring Break

Over spring break, my daughter was working on a school project about leaves, so I thought I'd offer to help her. From our third-floor balcony, I was surrounded by palm trees, and I could see our kids swimming in the hotel pool, so I yelled down, "Do you want me to get a palm-tree leaf for your collection?" Embarrassed because all the guests looked at her and then to me, she reluctantly nodded yes.

I reached over and pulled on a leaf. It came off – but so did 1,000 wasps, who seemed to want to sting only my left eye. I fell backwards and started screaming. My husband, who had been in the shower, came rushing out in a towel and was now screeching and swatting at the wasps as a group gathered below to watch.

We both ended up in the hospital for several hours. We were released but had giant welts on us. We looked so terrible that we skipped all of the excursions we had planned. The kids just played in the pool all week. After all the pain and suffering, I forget to take the palm leaf back home for my daughter.

~ A.D.

When in Rome

Shortly after we were married, my husband and I were on a Mediterranean cruise. Most of the people on the ship were twenty to thirty years older than us so it was difficult finding "dinner friends." After a few days of meals and excursions, though, we met two (older) couples that we really clicked with.

When we docked in Mykonos, Greece, the scheduled excursion was to visit the ruins, but my husband and I opted to skip that in favor of renting bikes and exploring the island on our own. We packed a blanket and snacks and headed out.

Late afternoon, when we were very hot and tired, we came across the beautiful, sparsely populated Elia Beach and parked our bikes and unpacked our blanket. Immediately my husband pointed out the obvious, "Everyone is naked!" followed by, "Take off your top!" I'm not the exhibitionist type, but all the beachgoers looked so relaxed and my hubs kept saying, "You don't know anyone here. Just take it off for a few minutes and we'll get in the water."

I agreed and removed my bikini top. Less than two seconds later, we heard, "Well, hello! We thought you were locals because I can see your boobs! You're naked! Bob, are you seeing this?" It was one of the husbands of the only two couples we knew on the ship. They all were staring at me as I stood there bare-breasted. Every night at dinner, the guy told the story to a new group of people, "We were just walking on the beach and wow! I saw her breasts up close. Her husband is a lucky man."
    ~ R.S.

No to Camp

For an introvert like me, a sleepover, middle-school camping trip at a new school was about the worst thing that could happen. I had to ride in a car with complete strangers, and I looked like a hairy beast because all the other girls were allowed to shave their legs and I wasn't.

To try and make a friend, I agreed to give one of the campers most of my money, thinking I wouldn't need it, as the camp was all-inclusive. I was left with only twenty dollars which would have been fine except our group leader never let us eat in the camp cafeteria. We went out for fast food every day and I didn't have enough money for meals. I was eating a small order of fries for lunch and dinner. We were camping in tents on the mountain when a torrential rain storm pounded on us, so they rushed all of us - fifty people - into a two-bed cabin.

I thought the week of hell was over when we got back in the car to head home, but the counselor/driver took a "shortcut" and we were two hours late. This was before cell phones, so my father was freaking out regarding his daughter's whereabouts, a matter only made worse when the counselor pulled the car up to his own home instead of the school parking lot.

I called my mother and she drove the thirty minutes to pick me up. Meanwhile, my suitcase had been put on a bus and taken back to the school parking lot because the car was too full to hold it. When my parents finally got my suitcase, it had been run over by the school bus, exploding my shampoo and sunscreen, which were smeared all over my undies and books. I never went on a school sleepover again.

~ Gretchen Davies
Author, *We're Only Human* and *The Obstinate Sheep*

The Blackout

I was traveling to San Francisco from Atlanta for work, and being a nervous flyer, I headed to the Crown Room to ease my anxiety with a cocktail. When my flight was delayed, I became more and more anxious and drank an additional cranberry juice with Tito's on the rocks until, finally, I boarded the plane.

I was so grateful that my eyes were getting heavy as I watched the flight attendant point out the closest exits. I was asleep before she even mentioned the snack cart. When the businessman next to me jostled me awake to wrestle the window blind open, the light blinded me. As I gave him the evil eye, I noticed we had landed.

Grabbing my cell phone out of my purse, I called my husband to let him know I had made it to California. Again, the businessman next to me was jostling me, this time poking his finger into my arm. "WHAT?" I yelled at him. "WHAT NOW?"

He smugly replied, "We are not in San Francisco. We haven't even taken off yet." Apparently, I had only been asleep for twenty minutes; the plane had not left the tarmac.

~ Jill

Wrestling on a Delta Flight

As a corporate trainer, I was assigned to help a group in Dallas for ten weeks, which required me to fly out every Sunday night and return Friday evenings. On one of these flights, I was stuck in one of the last rows. The gentleman seated in the aisle seat and I (seated by the window) exchanged smiles, and no other passengers were headed our way. We were thinking we had the luxury of an empty seat between us.

We both were adjusting our headphones when a giant, sweaty businessman waving his ticket stub around announced, "I'm B, I'm seat B!" The aisle-guy stood up to let him in. As seat-B guy tried to squeeze in, drops of sweat dripped down his face. He then turned his body to face the seat – to the dismay of the entire row in front of us as he jostled their seats forward as he tried to settle his almost seven-foot tall frame into the middle seat. He wasn't obese, he was just huge.

Seat-B guy huffed and puffed and then turned and plopped down between us. "I can't sit like this. It hurts," he declared, and moved my armrest to the upright position. He turned to aisle guy, who was leaning his body onto the armrest in resistance. They grappled for a minute, seat-B guy pulling the armrest up and the aisle guy pushing it down. They only stopped when I squealed after seat-B guy's body was crushing me against the wall.

Seat-B guy was breathing heavily and now outraged that the aisle-guy would not lift his armrest to accommodate his girth. "I'm sorry, but I can't fit in here," he said calmly. Then to the rest of the plane he announced, "I'm just big and tall," which was true but not a solution to our issue. "I paid for this whole seat, you can't have half of my seat," the aisle-guy reasoned. He continued, "I know the rules, you can't encroach on other passenger's seats. This is encroachment." "I normally fly business class, this is a mix up," seat-B seat guy insisted.

They both looked at me for some sort of decision. I said nothing, and they continued to stare at me. I looked to aisle-guy and then to seat-B guy with equal amount of compassion, yet concern. They grew tired of my lack of response and both started hitting the flight attendant call button at the same time.

Finally, a flight attendant appeared, and something remarkable happened. They didn't argue with one another but ganged up against the airline. It was as if they had strategized their position beforehand, like in-cahoots trial lawyers. "The airline messed up my seat," reasoned seat-B guy. "His femur is literally too long to fit in the seat" the aisle-guy pleaded. As the announcement for our seats to be in upright position and our tables raised, the flight attendant looked at me. I felt compelled to help and threw in, "It could be a safety issue," to the delight of my row mates, who were nodding in agreement.

The attendant motioned for them to both follow her. I was slightly jealous that they both moved to first class seats, but at least I had row 37 all to myself.

~ Ron D.

Threshold

I loved that my soon-to-be-husband, Mike, was getting a kick out of researching marriage customs. As our beach-wedding date approached, he would ask me if I was sure I didn't want to add the Celtic tradition of handfasting to our ceremony - where the bride and groom tie their hands together (hence the phrase "tying the knot") - or have our guests break plates that we would then clean up together to ward off evil spirits as the Germans do. I declined his ideas, staying with my mother and grandmothers' more American traditions of something borrowed, something blue.

Even so, I wasn't surprised after the wedding and reception when my husband wanted to carry me across the threshold. He explained that it started as an ancient Roman tradition to protect the bride from demons that could enter through her feet. I agreed we could try this one, but as we entered the honeymoon cottage, we found a steep, narrow set of steps. Undaunted, Mike turned me sideways and started up the steps.

About halfway up, my shoe got caught in the rail, which did not only abruptly stop his progress but caused him to drop to his knees. I told him he could put me down, but he refused. "NEVER!" he said as he got back up and continued to climb. Finally, we arrived at the top, where there was a little landing and a door. I awkwardly fought my large, puffy gown to find the door handle and unlocked it. Mike said, "Wait," and kissed me before we walked in.

He pushed the door open only to discover that it was a large utility closet containing the water heater and HVAC equipment. Mike turned around and carried me all the way back down the steps to find the bedroom on the main floor, just past the steps.

~ Shannon

Dare Devil

I'm from Indiana and begged my parents to let me go skiing with friends in Colorado. They were worried that I would get injured, as I had never skied before. I told them I would stay on the bunny slopes and spend a lot of time in the lodge. The first day we all skied, I opted to try a bigger slope and broke my leg. I spent the rest of the week by myself at the lodge. My parents still remind me of the incident twenty years later.

~ Jaime G.

Yes. I Do Remember That Trip.

The worst vacation of my life started with a Benadryl/Robitussin/Advil combo because I thought I had a cold. This was followed by an eight-hour road trip to South Carolina, a Medieval Times reservation, strawberry daiquiris served in a giant fish bowl, hurling into hedges, and a pastor. It ended at a twenty-four-hour clinic with diagnoses of dehydration, a double ear infection, pink eye, and walking pneumonia. I still have the pictures.

~ Colleen Salling

The first time I waded into the Atlantic Ocean, I walked directly into a giant jellyfish, which wrapped itself around both my legs. It looked like I'd been bullwhipped a hundred times from butt to toes. I spent the rest of the vacation watching the entire Harry Potter film series in bed, rotating cool towels, meat tenderizer, and iced tea bags to ease the pain.

~ Jo C.

No Excuse!

Even though my husband had only been in his new job for less than a year, he had such great numbers that they invited us to join the expense-paid, President's Club weekend at The Four Seasons in Newport Beach, California. Because our travel arrangements were made at the last minute and the flight was full, my husband and I weren't sitting in the same row. I was mid-plane and he was toward the back. A few of his coworkers were also on the plane, as they were flying from a huge sales appointment in Atlanta to the weekend event.

I was very pregnant while on this trip, so the second the seat-belt light went off and I was able to recline my seat, I did so, as the baby was sitting extremely low and I was uncomfortable sitting upright. As I pushed the chair back, I heard, "Jesus!" and then fingers appeared to the right and left of my head as the man behind me shook my seat.

"Move up! Move up!" he screamed. Apparently, my reclined seat had smooshed his laptop into his lap.

"I can't! I'm pregnant!" I said to the ceiling since I was not able to get up and turn to face him head-on.

The other passengers immediately shamed him, saying "She's pregnant!" and "Don't be an asshole!" My seat shook violently again as he got up and stuck his head close to mine. He whispered, "This is bullshit."

Upon our arrival in California, while I was sitting on one suitcase looking for our hotel voucher and my husband was waiting for the others on the carousel, I heard from behind me, "Shit, this giant pregnant woman was laying on me."

As I stood to confront him about his lack of consideration, my husband swung our last bag off the carousel, set it down, and said, "Hey, honey, this is my boss, John."

He tried to make it up to me all weekend by asking a hundred times if he could get me a drink, oblivious to the fact that each and every time I said I couldn't drink because I was pregnant.

~ Dolores Delaney

Double No

As a kid, my parents forced me to go camping. On the first day, I fell asleep when we were at the lake and got badly burned on my back. I was fevered, because of the burn. In the middle of the night, my mother, trying to help stabilize my body temperature, opened the tent flaps and propped the tent door open, hoping for a breeze. The next morning, I had 10,000 mosquito bites all over my sunburned back. I was so sore, I couldn't move, and we still had six days of vacation left.

~ NG

Apologies, I Was Confused

When my wife and I were in Australia for a biotech conference, we visited a few of the vineyards in the area during our free time and noticed that even the more expensive wines had twist-off tops, which we associated with cheaper wines. The sommelier launched into a detailed explanation of why twist-off caps are not inferior to traditional corks, going on and on about the tannin levels in red wines versus white wines, how some wines did not need oxygen oxidation, and finally the shortage of Quercus suber trees in Spain and Portugal. Net-net, screw-off tops are becoming the rage for many vineyards. We bought a few bottles and headed to the hotel to get ready for the evening's big company dinner.

My wife and I were running a few minutes late, and when we found our assigned seating, the waiter was pouring a glass of wine for the gentleman next to me. I heard him tell the man next to him that his father actually had won a Nobel Peace Prize for his findings in "corks." Trying to make conversation, I chimed in that the study of corks was quite fascinating and recounted the events of the day about the oxidation process and the shortage of *Quercus suber* trees.

The two gentlemen looked confused, almost angry. One insisted, "We are talking about corks.'"

I said, "Yes, corks."

He replied, "Coooooorks."

I nodded and looked at my wife, like "What the hell is wrong with this guy? I know a lot about corks. Why is he being so weird?"

"QUARKS!" he screamed at me. "The subatomic particles carrying a fractional electric charge, postulated as building blocks of the hadrons!"

"OHHH," I said. "Quarks, I thought you said 'corks.'" My wife lifted her glass to me and we only talked to each other the rest of the evening.

~ Mark

I'm Going to be Sick

I was in Atlanta and headed to a wedding in San Francisco. We had barely taken off when I heard someone throwing up behind me. At the last minute, the man stood up, trying to squeeze out of the window seat to the aisle. He didn't make it and projectile-vomited onto my entire row. In between his hurls, he kept saying, "My bad. My bad."

~ Sharon

Not in the Smocking

My in-laws were from a long line of Northeastern well-to-do's, so their son and I were outcasts as public-school teachers in middle America. Nonetheless, they were family, and we made our obligatory pilgrimage to visit them during the holidays.

We were flying with our three-year-old and five-month-old, making the short two-hour trip from Chicago to Manhattan, when the pilot announced the plane would be rerouted to deplane and reboard in Pittsburgh and then go on to LaGuardia. As the plane started to descend in Pittsburgh, the baby's diaper exploded. I was wearing a fancy dress and the baby was in a Strasburg's heirloom-looking white romper - complete with fabric-covered buttons and tucks - white socks, and soft saddle-shoe-style footies to impress the Ivy League in-laws. We were completely drenched in green poo.

My husband, seated in the aisle over, stood up to get the diaper bag but was told, "Sit down, sir! We are landing!"

"My baby's covered in poop!" my husband replied, and the attendants seemed to have no concern for that.

The coach seat was so tight I could barely stretch the baby out to take off his clothes. The poo kept coming out in violent squirts, accompanied by shrieks from the woman in the window seat beside me. Passengers were gagging all around us, and United Airline blankets and cocktail napkins came flying up the aisle to help with the cleanup.

The smell of baby diarrhea and vomit made me nauseous, and because I had used the air-sickness bags as wipes, I threw up in the aisle. Passengers were yelling "Holy shit!" and other expletives as our three-year-old reminded me, "That is not a nice word. Mommy, he is saying bad words."

Exiting the plane, my husband looked like a Tibetan Sherpa struggling with the two car seats, a stroller and our luggage. I held the five-month-old wrapped in only an airline blanket while our toddler held on to my dress. Just when I thought I had the baby settled in the Pittsburgh airport, he would poop again. He had gone through the emergency outfits in the diaper bag, and I did not have access to my luggage. On top of that, I reeked of breast milk and poo. I instructed my husband to buy us fresh clothing, and he did his best.

When we finally reboarded the next flight and made it to New York, my in-laws were not impressed with my or the baby's outfit selection. I was sporting an oversized Steelers Super Bowl sweatshirt and pajama bottoms; the five-month-old had a onesie paying tribute to Jerome Bettis, The Bus, the superstar running back.

My mother-in-law said nothing until we got to the car. She whispered to my father-in-law, "They don't allow pajama bottoms at the club."
~ S.A.S.

Thank You for Coming, Never Come Back

My husband and I, plus our good friends, Amy and John, were traveling to Vegas for the weekend to see a Kenny Chesney concert and visit with my parents who had recently moved to Sin City. The morning of the concert we all enjoyed a lovely brunch of Eggs Benedict and mimosas and decided, since we had the whole day, to attend the musical *Rock of Ages* at The Venetian, which features glam metal bands of the 1980's.

The six of us (my parents, Amy and John, plus Bill and I) settled into our seats - which were fourth-row center. The crowd was well dressed and calm, as one would expect at a matinee musical. A third of the way into it, the four people seated in the row directly in front of us jumped up and started waving their arms and dancing to Styx's "Too Much Time On My Hands". It was as if whatever drug they had taken had kicked in full force. Not one other person in the entire theatre was standing or dancing, but we gave them some grace since it was an upbeat song. They continued to stand through Bon Jovi's "Dead Or Alive".

Our group, and frankly, the audience members behind us started to get annoyed when they continued to rock out to the slow songs such as Night Ranger's "Sister Christian" and Reo Speedwagon's "I Can't Fight This Feeling" which motivated us to tap them politely, and ask if they would please sit down because no one could see the show behind them. They ignored us and continued to dance for the remainder of the show.

When the lights came up, one of the dancing women turned to us and said, "It's a rock concert, you f*****g bitches." At that point my husband ran out of the aisle, only to be stopped by one of the dancing men. The guy, who was dressed nicely in a white Oxford shirt, trousers and dress shoes, got in my husband's face and asked, "Do you want a piece of this?", and proceeded to chest bump him. Bill clocked him in the jaw, and it was game-on.

I ran to try to break it up. As I was pulling Bill off, the guy in the Oxford shirt took another swing, missing Bill and hitting me so hard in the head, I fell to the floor. It was at this point, even though it was brunch time and I was decked out in my new off one shoulder Helmut Lang dress that I realized in the question of "Flight or Fight," I was a fighter. By the time I got up my dad had jumped into it and had oxford guy in a solid choke hold while Bill joined John to defend Amy from the other couple. I saw Amy chucking her soda bottle and snacks at the perpetrators while everyone was shoving and pointing fingers.

I pulled at the guy's oxford, twisting it tight, and as his face was turning blue, I yelled, "How dare you, I'm a mom of three little kids and this is their grandpa you mother -f****r!"

"Security" showed up, which consisted of guys with whistles, saying, "Stop it," in between whistling.

Finally, we were all taken outside, and the hotel staff was very apologetic, sharing with us that witnesses had stated the two couples had provoked the whole thing and they were sorry. Oddly, when they walked us out to the parking lot, they read us something from a small laminated card that sounded sort of like Miranda Rights, but in place of, "You have the right to remain silent," they informed us that we were never allowed in the Venetian or any Sands owned resort in the world, forever. Bill told them that was fine because we don't stay in their hotels anyway, we were at the Hard Rock Hotel.

The next morning, Bill went to get the paper and exchanged looks with my dad, who was all dressed up in a suit because he was headed to a business meeting. They both smiled, as each had busted lips and bruised knuckles from the night before.

~ Jenny and Bill Tadio

OUTFIT FAILS

Always make new mistakes.

~ Ester Dyson

I Can See Your Business

My husband and I were staying with friends at their beautiful beach house in Santa Rosa for our final getaway before "the babies," as I was expecting twins within the next few weeks. My friend Audrey's two toddlers were taking swimming lessons in the neighborhood pool in the mornings, and by ten, the temperature had already swelled to ninety. Audrey told me to bring my swimsuit; she said we could sit on the opposite side of pool from where they were taking their lessons and then hang at the pool until lunch.

I protested, saying I was so fat, but when Audrey gave me one of her one-piece maternity bathing suits, an oversized cover-up and a floppy hat, I acquiesced because I was already sweating and the idea of floating appealed to me, as I was carrying close to eighty pounds of extra weight.

All went well with the lessons, and we decided to extend our stay to enjoy lunch at the pool. Eventually, I had to use the restroom, so Audrey and I gathered up the toddlers and headed to the potty. I started to panic when I couldn't get the bathing suit off; it was wet and stuck to my body, not to mention I was having trouble maneuvering myself in the confines of the tiny bathroom stall.

I voiced my concerns to Audrey, who calmly replied, "Just pee through the suit and then shower off. That's what I used to do." I explained that I had more than a pee situation going on. "Just yank the suit to the side of your business."

I yanked, sat down, completed my business, washed my hands and headed back to the patio chairs. I needed to dry out if I ever wanted to escape the bathing suit.

I had a book in my hand and my legs propped up when everyone who passed by me—Audrey and the kids included—looked mortified.

Audrey threw a towel over my bottom half, saying, "You have toilet paper stuck to the inside of your thigh."

I exhaled and said, "Goodness, everyone was looking at me as if I was nude."

Audrey held up one finger and continued, "And your suit is only halfway back into position and we all saw your vagina."
~ Marie Arcuri

Why I Should Not Wear Heels

I was headed off to work in my usual uniform, a pantsuit and high heels. Because my baby was still in the bucket car carrier, I had to make two trips to load my laptop bag, purse, lunch, and a large gym bag. Our house is a ranch built into a hill, so the garage/basement is down one flight of wooden stairs with spaces in between each step. There is no wall on the left side, just a handrail attached to a support beam.

As I headed down the steps, the heel of my right foot

caught the hem of my pants and projected my body forward. I was not holding onto the railing because I was carrying all my gear and I saw my life flash before my eyes. It happened SO FAST. I remember hitting my upper left arm on something hard, then my head struck the ceiling above the end of the staircase, and VOILA! I was at the bottom of the stairs on my feet! I could not believe that I only suffered a big bump on my head and a bruised arm. For years after that, I only wore flats.

~ Brooke Fowler
    Married AF podcast

I Hate Snakes
I was sitting on the toilet and happened to look down to see a snake in the bowl. I jumped up - almost hurting myself - screamed and moved away from the bowl. It was then that I realized there was no snake in the toilet. It was the tie from my cardigan.

~ Jessica Van Derven
    Writer, WisconsinTrophyWife.com

Skinny Jeans Are Dangerous
I had recently lost weight and wanted to celebrate with new jeans, so I headed to the mall with my husband, Jim, and our youngest daughter. Every style I picked out my daughter objected to, she handed me a few pairs and we headed to the dressing room.

I was putting on the first pair when I realized the jeans

were super, super-stretchy. My daughter, in the room with me, trying on a pair of similar fabric, insisted that was the style, "They're skinny jeans." Just hearing the word skinny motivated me to muscle them on.

I grabbed the belt loops on either side and, as I gave a firm tug and jumped up enough to get the jeans over my feet, my heel caught the bottom the pants. As I came down, I knew I was off balance and contorted myself to fall away from my daughter.

I must have turned my foot in the process because when I came down, I heard my foot "pop." I had snapped my foot in half - the fifth metatarsal bone. I was not allowed to drive, had my foot in a cast for six weeks, and gained back all the weight. Skinny jeans are made by the devil.
~ Susan Holloway

Ho, Ho, No...
Someone just told me they loved my "ugly Christmas sweater," but it was just one of my regular sweaters.
~ Angie Brogan

THE GRASS IS NOT GREENER

Like a good neighbor,
stay over there.
~ Unknown

It's on Sale

I'm not proud of this, but for a time in college, I was smoking a lot of weed. I smoked so much that I always had a lot a weed, and sort of by accident, I became a ... distributor. At the time, it was perfect because my part-time drug-dealer job financed my weed habit and extracurricular activities, such as concerts and road trips.

Things were going great until my car died. It was a junker, an old Buick with floorboards rusted out so badly that, if the floor mat moved, you could see the road. I was very upset because I was planning on taking a new lady friend that I had met in chemistry lab to see the band Whitesnake.

My new neighbor, Todd, came over and asked me if he could buy a lot of my "product" on credit. I said no. [Life lesson: Never give stoners credit. They won't pay you back.] He begged and whined about having company over, saying he really wanted to be a great host. I ignored his pleas. He left in a huff, screaming, "Just wait one minute." He returned, jingling keys, announcing that he would trade his truck for a generous portion of product. I agreed, and we traded.

The truck was a rust bucket. The passenger-side mirror was taped on with duct tape. You could not roll down the windows because they would never go back up, and there was a large hole in the driver's door. In spite of the horrific condition of the vehicle, Todd told me with a straight face,

"The left taillight doesn't work, so you should fix that."

I packed a cooler with beer and weed, and my date and I were off in my new/used clunker. Right before we were about to turn into the venue, police lights came on behind me. I pulled over and grabbed my license out of my wallet.

The police officer started yelling, "Please exit the car with your hands up, please exit the car with your hands up." I slowly opened the door and lifted my hands in the air. My date was crying uncontrollably. "This car is stolen," the officer said flatly.

I was sitting in a jail cell with a few other guys, discussing my charges: possession of an illegal substance and stealing a piece of shit Isuzu truck with rotting, rusted sides.

A fellow inmate, Wayne, stopped me. "What color's the truck?" I replied it might be white, but it was so rusty, I wasn't sure. Wayne said, "That sounds like my truck. It was stolen."

My neighbor had traded me a stolen car. Eventually, the stolen-vehicle charge was dropped and the drug charge was brought down to a misdemeanor because I agreed to rehab and community service.

The original reason I was pulled over? It was for the broken left taillight.

~ Kyle F.

Election Night

Our new neighbor, Ben, was a hotshot political consultant. He bragged about how he had kept a congressman in office for twenty years despite scandals with booze, women and other tawdry behavior. On election night, he invited our entire block to join him at a local sports bar to watch the results, which came in around eleven. His precious incumbent lost. Everyone left the bar to head home, including Ben's wife, but Ben stayed, saying he had to make some calls.

Later, around 4:00 a.m., our phone rang. It was Sarah, Ben's wife, saying someone was in her home. The children were there, and she was very frightened and waiting for the police. My wife and I jumped out of bed and headed over to their house. On the way we passed many mailboxes that had been knocked over, the end of a retaining wall that had been smashed, and finally, a crashed, unfamiliar Jeep.

We showed up to Sarah's at the same time two police cars arrived and told them about the Jeep. Everyone was in a panic that the driver had broken into Sarah's home, so Sarah and her children joined us on the lawn while the police, guns drawn, entered the house. A few minutes later, they appeared with Ben.

He had been so drunk he couldn't find his own car keys, and he borrowed a car from the bartender. He drove wildly through the neighborhood, striking many objects, entered the house by using the garage code, and then proceeded to pull down the attic steps, climbed in and passed out.

Ben's shady congressman was not the only one that lost that night. Sarah filed for divorce and their lovely four-bedroom, five-bath Cape Cod with a pool is currently on the market.

~ C.C.

It's Not What You Think

It was a Sunday and we were unpacking moving boxes in our new home. I had evidently marked a few of the crates incorrectly because we were missing all the kitchen utensils as well as my husband's and my pajamas. We did find a box of adult onesies that we had been given as a gift and that we sometimes wore during the holidays. One was a bunny, with ears on the hood and a little tail; the other was Batman, with the cape.

We put on the onesies and made a pact not to change out of them until every last box was unloaded and put away. We were in the home office, finally getting to the last of the unpacking. My husband was sitting at the desk, holding several cords in each hand as he put the computer back together, while I sat on the floor, going through files. The trash can was on his side, but his hands were occupied, so I was leaning over him to throw away some old papers right when the doorbell rang.

My head popped up - from what looked like my husband's lap - and we both turned to see our neighbors looking at us in shock. Catching us in our onesies, in that position, they must have thought we were into some sort of sexual furry/superhero fetish.

We waved, but they barely lifted their heads in a nod. My husband said, through the glass, "I'm coming around!"

The man pointed to his watch and said, "We've caught you at a bad time."

They turned and hustled down the driveway, not even leaving the casserole, which stinks because we had just found the utensils.

~ Lisa B

Bird-Watching

I schedule my bath for the same time my super-hot neighbor takes his shower. His house is down the hill from mine, so I can see him, but he can't see me. I keep binoculars by the tub.

My husband asked, "Why do you have binoculars?"

I replied, "Birds."

~ Kathy C

Night Swimming

Our neighbor who lived two doors down developed a reputation for hosting parties and then, at around 1:00 a.m., he would emerge from his powder room completely naked, except for goggles. He would sprint to the community's pool, and the only thing he would say as he left was, "Party in the pool!"

No one ever joined him.

~ V.V.

You're Not off the Hook

I've nicknamed two of our neighbors "Jerry" and "Donna," after Grateful Dead band members because they encourage their offspring to be free-spirited. They allow their kids and their children's friends to drink and smoke dope on their property. I rarely open my bedroom windows on the second floor for fear of getting high.

Our son was home from college for the weekend and said he was going to go hang out with Jerry and Donna's crew. His sister (our daughter) said, "Don't go over there. They're drug dealers."

The word got out about the drug-dealing accusation and texts started flying amongst our kids and the neighbor's children. Finally, the oldest of Jerry and Donna's kids was passing by as we were getting into our car. He stopped, rolled down his window, and addressed us.

"Mr. and Mrs. Walters, I'm not a drug dealer. That's a rumor that I sell drugs. I want you to know that I have never sold drugs to your kids. I have always given them weed for free."

~ M. Sewell

You Are in Violation

We were so excited to be moving from the Northeast into a suburban community in Georgia as everyone we met while house hunting went out of their way to extend Southern hospitality. Within days of moving into our new house, however, we learned that the main street that ran front to back in the middle of the neighborhood had been renamed "The Miserable Mile." Three of the families that lived along the street were at war with one another over issues such as yard violations, negligent pet owners not scooping up after their dogs, and a bullying child who tormented other kids on the school bus.

I took the gossip with a grain of salt until I pulled into the neighborhood one day and saw four police cars. Slowly, I passed by a yard where three women and two men were in each other's faces, pointing fingers and screaming. One man came from the garage and physically picked up his wife, potato-sack style, and carried her into their house. By morning, the word was out about how the altercation started.

One couple had warned the other couple multiple times about leaving their garden hose out, within view, which was a violation of the HOA covenants. The couple retaliated by saying that other neighbors had visible garden hoses and were not getting violation notices, so they would not accept the notices and not remove the hose from view. From there, it escalated into the brawl.

Our house is for sale. We're moving to a farm.
~ Sandi

NOT SO HAPPY BIRTHDAY

Just because you fail once
doesn't mean you're gonna
fail at everything.
~ Marilyn Monroe

You Give Alcohol A Bad Name

For my fortieth birthday, my friends treated me to a night out to watch a Bon Jovi tribute band. The bar was featuring what they said was Jon Bon Jovi's favorite drink, the Muff Dive, which is vodka, Kahula and Baileys Irish Cream. The crowd treated me to several drinks, enough to feel confident to rush the stage to confiscate lookalike guitarist Richie Sambora's hat. Security did not think the theft of the Royal Flush by Stetson knock-off was amusing and escorted me off the stage and to the parking lot to sober up.

~ Peri Sue

On my tenth birthday, I bent over to blow out the candles and my hair caught on fire. I was fine, just my ends were scorched.

~ Allison Woods

I'll never forget my 52nd birthday. I was awake all night passing a kidney stone.

~ Noel Taylor

Why Thank You

I skipped work and enjoyed a spa day with a good friend for my birthday. We got complete makeovers and were feeling fabulous when we stepped into Marlow's Tavern to get a drink. The bar was busy, so we grabbed a table. The waiter was super-cute and complimented me. He asked, "Have you ever modeled?" I blushed, because I do not handle compliments well and I flipped my hair while shaking my head "no". He asked again if I had modeled? I said, "Don't be silly, we just had our hair and nails done today." My friend looked at me with the strangest cringed face. When the waiter asked a third time, "Have you ever done any modeling?" he seemed annoyed. Before I could answer my friend said, "Yes. We've been to Marlow's. Can we order a drink?" The waiter was asking if I had ever been to a Marlowe's, not if I had ever been a model.

~ Jen B.

It's My Birthday

For twenty-six solid years I provided constant reminders to my family and friends - at least a month in advance - that my birthday was coming on August fourth. I did not do household chores on MY birthday. I picked the breakfast, lunch, and dinner meals on MY birthday. That all changed when I turned twenty-seven and gave birth to my son on the same day.

~ Whitney Zaeh Watts

Check Please

My mom flew out to Los Angeles to celebrate my 32nd birthday, and I planned a nice get-together with a few of my friends at Buca di Beppo's at Universal Studios. I arrived with my mom and my boyfriend a few minutes early. No one else had arrived yet, but my mom had gifted me a giant birthday hat that I excitedly put on.

An hour later, no one had arrived. We were at a large table, and I was still wearing the birthday hat and telling the waiter that we did not want to order because we were expecting a big group. We waited and waited. I was heartbroken and trying not to cry. (This was pre-cell phone days, so I couldn't call to check to see where everyone was.) Finally, we went home, and the phone rang. My friends were all at a different Buca di Beppo's.

~ Barbara Leimkuehler

Well, Hello Officer

My husband threw me a surprise birthday party for my fortieth. It got a little crazy - people were dancing on the lawn furniture and taking off their bras and burning them in the fire pit. When two attractive men arrived in police uniforms, I greeted them, jumping up and down and asking, "Are you my strippers? MY STRIPPERS ARE HERE!" They were not strippers. The neighbors had called the cops to report the loud music.

~ Heather Hobson Terry

When we were dating, my husband, Scott, bought me lingerie as one of my birthday gifts, which seemed like something that he would benefit from more than I would. In February, on his birthday, he was surprised with one of his gifts, a new Kate Spade handbag.

~ Carol Arbors

BACK TO SCHOOL

Success is always
less funny than failure.
~ Jon Robinson

I Love America

When I was in high school, my parents signed up to host a Yugoslavian exchange student named Dragutin for the weekend because our city was a midpoint for wherever he was going for the rest of the summer. When I was supposed to pick him up from Marietta College at 3:00 a.m., I was leaving a party with my friend, Robbie, and heading to another party across town.

We were driving the speed limit when a car started riding our bumper. Robbie tapped the brakes a few times, but the guy would not let up. In frustration, I rolled down the window and chucked a full beer can at the car, which exploded with great effect on the grill. I celebrated for one whole second before the red and blue lights came on. I had struck a sheriff's car. They pulled us over and instructed us to report to the police station at 8:00 a.m. the next morning (this was in the 1980s in a small town).

I woke up, with my mother an inch from my face, screaming at me about Dragutin. "Where's Dragutin?" She paused and furiously added, "I know where he is! He's upstairs, exhausted and confused because YOU left him at the college!"

After the screaming stopped, I remembered that I was supposed to be at the police station and it was now close to noon. My mother instructed me to get Dragutin and not let him out of my sight for the rest of the weekend. So,

Dragutin (whom my friends and I called Dragon), Robbie and I headed to the police station.

We were assigned roadside trash pickup duty on Route 60, orange suits and all. As we poked trash with our sticks and stuck them into canvas bags, our friends drove by, honking and waving at us. Robbie and I would never wave back, but Dragon waved vigorously to every vehicle. Once we finished our trash-pickup duty, Robbie and I took Dragon to a waffle restaurant and then back home to watch movies because I was grounded.

Dragon was soon off to a bigger city to enjoy what would be a real cultural experience, visiting historical sites and museums, maybe a baseball game or other things that are considered American. But for several years, even when I had graduated from college, my mom would send me letters from Dragutin. He would write about what he was doing in his life and he would always thank me for his wonderful memories – when he was with me and Robbie, visiting an American police station and eating waffles.

~ P.C.

Turn on Your Spell Check

The entire second grade was headed to the city aquarium for a field trip, and the two hundred students were given bright-orange Tiger Elementary shirts so the teachers and chaperones could easily spot the kids in the massive facility. The night before the aquarium adventure, the second-grade teacher that was in charge of the event sent a reminder email about the shirts. It read: "Thank you for buying the shits. It is important that your child wear their shit tomorrow on the field trip, as the aquarium hosts thousands of students daily and we want to create a safe environment for your child. If you still have not purchased a shit, we have a few available, come into the office tomorrow before 7:30 am if you want to purchase the orange field trip shit."

Shortly after sending that email, he sent this one: "Apologies for calling shirts shits in my previous email."
~ S.K.

I Don't Love You, So Much
I got off the middle-school bus at my friend's house and a girl stood up and started taunting me about liking her friend. "You love Debra! You love Debra!" I kept telling her to shut up, but she would not stop. In a moment of anger, I grabbed my book bag and hurled it toward the bus window – I wanted to scare her by hitting the glass with the pack. Unfortunately, I overthrew, and it landed on top of the bus. The bus drove away, and even though my friends and I were chasing it, I never saw that book bag again.
~ Steven Paints

I'm Resting
In 1990, in the outskirts of Columbus, Ohio, the only restaurant open twenty-four hours a day was the Krystal, so my friend Tim and I headed over at 3:00 a.m. It was

freezing cold and snowing heavily when we made it to the drive-thru and ordered our food. We pulled forward and cranked up the heat, but the wait was really long and Tim and I both passed out.

We were woken by an enormous police officer pounding on the passenger-side window (seeing us asleep and surrounded by empty beer cans) yelling, "Get out of this car or I'm going to give you both a DUI!" We shuffled to the police car and he let us use his phone to call a friend to drive us home. We waited, for what seemed like hours, for our ride. The officer never said one word to us the whole time we were in the car.

When our ride arrived, he said, "Just wait a minute!" Tim and I both thought he had changed his mind and was taking us to jail. "Did you order food?" he asked. We nodded and told him we had ordered bags of burgers. "You damn well better pay for it," he said.
    ~ P.C.

My kid packed an entire box of ice cream sandwiches in their lunch bag.
    ~ K.T.

My Bad

One day after school, some students were working very hard to raise awareness for the upcoming Child Abuse Prevention Week by making posters to be displayed in all the halls of our middle school. I was happy the kids were engaged in the project, as it allowed me to catch up on grading papers. The kids taped their posters in the hallway just before the parents rolled through to see their artwork. I was devastated to see that many students had taken liberties and abbreviated Child Abuse Prevention Week. Many of the signs read: "CHILD ABUSE WEEK." It was the most humiliating moment in my 30+ year career. I added "PREVENTION" on every poster with a red sharpie.

~ Lee St. John
Author, *SHE'S A KEEPER! Teacher Stories from Real Southern Classrooms*

It All Started with the Fungus

On a camping trip with three buddies at Letchworth State Park, we decided to take mushrooms for the first time. While the mushrooms were kicking in, we designed a campfire with a base and ring of rocks, and then gathered a lot of twigs, dry leaves and a few larger logs to start it. We sat on our rolled-up sleeping bags and were enjoying the sun going down, overlooking the amazing river that could be seen from the steep gorge next to where we had settled.

The mushrooms had just started to kick in when we thought we were being bombed. The fire was exploding, over and over again. We were kicking dirt over the flames, trying to extinguish it, but it continued to blast for several minutes. When the night finally quieted, one of my friends, a previous Boy Scout, remembered that you were never supposed to use "wet or porous stones in a fire because they can detonate." It is unfortunate that he recalled that information only after we had built the fire pit and we were all high. In the chaos, we had kicked our rolled backpacks into the gorge and lost all our belongings - including the rest of our drugs - and had to hike several miles back to our car in complete darkness on steep, rocky terrain.

~ Luke

Catch You Later

There was a local guy, Rick, who owned at least twenty car dealerships around town. He was famous for his commercial jingles that seemed to play nonstop on television. Rick had been in my fraternity, thirty years before me. On game days, he would generously show up to the fraternity house with kegs of beer or he would buy our whole group pizza, so he could relive his glory days.

After a full day of drinking, he was unfit to drive and asked me to drive him home. He flipped me his keys - they were to a Ferrari. I grabbed my buddy, Tim, and we headed out. Less than a block away from campus - and before he told us his address - he passed out. He had a bag phone (this was before cell phones were common) in his car, which we used to call information to reach his wife. We secured the address and delivered him through the security gates of a palatial estate. Tim and I helped him out of the car and walked/dragged him to the door, where his wife was waiting on the porch.

"Just where the hell has he been?" she asked. He woke up at that moment and said, "Oh hi, honey." Then he looked at us, back at the car and slurred, "Keep it for a few days."

For two weeks, my fraternity brothers and I took turns driving the Ferrari to pick up dates or to get takeout Chinese food. Eventually, two men from the dealership came to pick it up. We still saw Rick at most home games.
~ P.C.

Oh, Hell No

The middle school had a reputation for perpetual carpool line-cutters and parking-spot stealers. The line-cutting and parking situations were so bad I created a Facebook page dedicated to the jerks who didn't follow the rules; I called it "Carpool Shamers." My friends and I would post pictures of cars cutting in line, as well as cars parked illegally in the fire lanes or in other people's spots. As a fundraiser for the PTA, the school auctioned off parking spaces to parents, and starting bids were $100. Bidding was furious, but I finally won a spot, paying $800.

The following morning, I was substituting at the middle school. My normally-hurried pace slowed, as I remembered I did not have to fight for a parking spot. As I pulled around to the front to my newly-minted parking space, adorned with my name on it, I was dismayed to see a minivan parked there. My phone was pinging before I could make another loop.

ASShat minivan is in your spot
10 minutes ago · Like

Holy s*** is someone really in your spot?
9 minutes ago · Like

WTF?
8 minutes ago · Like

n Seriously? YOUR NAME IS ON THE SPOT
7 minutes ago · Like

g HEADS WILL ROLL!
6 minutes ago · Like

s This site is immature and ridiculous.
You should find something better to do with your time. Take this
site down immediately.
5 minutes ago · Like

No!
4 minutes ago · Like

g First ammendment!
3 minutes ago · Like

s You cannot make us take it down. Can she make
us take it down?
2 minutes ago · Like

n No!
2 minutes ago · Like

We did not take the page down, but my substitute-teaching opportunities slowed to a crawl.

~ Anonymous

Teacher's Revenge

When the sixth graders at my school were studying ancient Greece in social studies, the teachers assigned each student their own Greek name, taking care to match the names with the students' personalities. A boy who farted incessantly received the name Pootacles and the two most annoying female students were named Obnoxia and Dyspepsia.

~ Lee St. John
Author, *SHE'S A KEEPER! Teacher Stories from Real Southern Classrooms*

IT'S YOUR HAIR

Call Me Tina

In seventh grade, I had the gift of wonderfully thick hair that I had grown out past the middle of my back. My mom wanted to trim the split ends, so she made a few snips across the back and handed me a mirror. It looked perfect. I asked her to trim the front a little to frame my face. At first, my hair was parted wrong, so she made a small correction, but in her pursuit to make it even, she kept trimming and trimming. She cut it so short it wouldn't stay down and spiked straight up like Tina Turner's 1984 "What's Love Got to Do with It" video. The kids at school called me Tina even after my bangs grew back.

~ Lori Hartman-Nona

In middle school, I wanted the Rachel Green sleek bob (from *Friends*, season seven) and ended up with the Carol Brady mullet.

~ Brittany Gerald

My mom, who had great hair of her own, use to wear wigs, "for fun." I would be mortified when she would show up to school one day with a brunette Dorothy Hamill style and then the next day with a blonde Marilyn Monroe.

~ Traci Jo

Many, Many Apologies

Note: This was not my proudest moment; the combination of my 50th birthday, many people waiting for me and the throws of menopause may have influenced my actions.

My husband had planned an enormous birthday party for me to celebrate my 50th. I went to the salon a few minutes early hoping to get in because I had an entire list of errands to run after. I waited over 20 minutes before asking a stylist if she had seen Marge. She had a weird look and went to get the manager. The manager told me that Marge could not do my hair. I told her I had made the appointment over a month ago and I had close to 100 people waiting for me - what is going on? The manager said, "She passed away." I was very sad to hear such terrible news and told her as such but asked why didn't they call me so I could reschedule the appointment? The manager replied, "Because it just happened today."

I hugged the manager and told her how sorry I was, Marge was a great stylist and a wonderful person. I would attend the service and send flowers. The manager said, "thank you" and hugged me again. I patted her hand and asked as nicely as I possibly could, "I have to be at the restaurant in less than an hour, is anyone available that could just help me with an up-do?"
  ~ Sandra Stinson

The Bang Trimmer
When I was within weeks of turning fifty, I decided to have long bangs cut into my hair, which had been one length all over. I provided the stylist with a picture of the exact cut I wanted, which showed long bangs that fell well past the nose.

The stylist asked, "Are you sure you really want bangs?"

I showed her the picture again and said, "Yes, like this - long bangs." In one swift movement, she drew my bangs up over my head and sliced them to within an inch of my scalp. "OH MY GOSH!" I screamed, waving the picture in front of her. "I wanted long bangs! See these bangs? They are long!"

"Sorry," she said calmly. "They'll look better after you wash them."
   ~ Sandi Stati

I Like the Old Me
I asked for a shoulder-length, layered style and ended up with a straight, chin-length bob. When I told my (former) stylist that it wasn't what I wanted, he paused, realized his error, and said, "It's the new you!"
   ~ Amy Green Meadows

Too Much
I had burned the ends of my hair with a bleach treatment and requested that the hairdresser cut what they could off the burned ends. When they were done, I looked up to see a severe bowl cut - like Lloyd Christmas from Dumb and Dumber.
   ~ Lori Hartman-Nona

MOM BRAIN

Trying is the first step
towards failure.
~ Homer Simpson

The Decade

When my husband and I were approaching our tenth wedding anniversary, I made a strong suggestion to my thrifty groom that we needed to do something BIG. I appreciated the cards and the dinners over the years, but a decade of marriage deserved something grand. I wanted a no-expenses-spared weekend away, and I was thrilled when he booked a lovely room in historic Savannah, overlooking the river, surprising me with tickets to all the tourist highlights as well. We visited antebellum homes, took a carriage ride, and reserved a table at Paula Deen's restaurant. We blissfully ate, drank, and shopped our way through the beautiful city.

Returning home to Atlanta, I was using my phone to give my mom a photographic tour of the beautiful homes, parks, and our meals when she said, "Wow, this was quite lavish for your anniversary." I told her we had earned it, hitting ten years of marriage.

She went over to the bookshelves and, picking up one of our wedding pictures that was etched with the date of our nuptials, and said flatly, "You've only been married for seven years, dear."

I still haven't told my husband; he thinks we're coming up on our 15th and I'm shooting for Europe.

~ Deanna G.

Hurry

My mom told me to stay in the car while she ran into the grocery store. We were expecting dinner guests in less than an hour and she could, "Handle things on her own much faster." Less than ten minutes later I saw her rushing out of the store, holding several bags on each arm. I was impressed until I watched her whip open the backseat door of the car parked directly across from us. She literally threw the groceries in, only realizing her mistake when the couple in the front seat screamed.

~ Carol

I Need a F*****g Break

Many years ago, when I had just given birth to my third son, I was on the brink of a mental breakdown. I was trying to handle a newborn plus two toddlers alone because my husband traveled during the week for work. On Sunday night, I was crying as he headed out to the airport. I was surprised - and relieved - when a few hours later, he was back. His flight had been canceled due to a political conflict in the country he was visiting, which was great news for me. He could work from home for a few days until he was reassigned, and I could escape for a few minutes.

Having just put the three boys down for a nap, I would have at least an hour before they woke, so I grabbed my purse and said, "I'm going to the grocery store, by myself." I headed to the minivan and was securing my seat belt when the side door opened: it was my husband, buckling the newborn's car seat in the van. "NO!" I said. "I need a break!"

"What if he cries? I can't feed him!" my husband said as he pointed to his chest.

"There are bottles in the refrigerator!" I screamed back.

As my husband and I silently stared at each other, I put the car into drive and headed to the store. I leisurely shopped for the week's meals, lingered in the bubble-bath section for at least ten minutes, and was feeling recharged when I headed back to the van. As I hit the key fob to open the trunk of the minivan, I dropped the groceries and screamed. I could see the baby I had forgotten in the backseat, sound asleep. Thank goodness it was fall and the weather was moderate; he was peacefully dreaming as I sobbed in the driver's seat.

When I walked in the front door, still hiccupping from crying, I tried to tell my husband the story. Within months, he quit his travel job.
~ Suzie Roukes

It's a Monday
I had already returned home once because I realized, as we pulled up to the elementary carpool line, one of the twins was missing a shoe. If I hurried, I could still get the twins dropped off and the toddler to preschool and only

be a few minutes late for the Monday morning meeting.

As I approached the daycare drop-off, I instructed Emily, my three-year-old, to gather her snack. She started asking, "Where's my water bottle? I can't go to school without my water bottle. It gets sooooo hot outside!" I felt around on the floor for a loose one to no avail. As the teacher opened the door to get Emily out, who was now wailing about not having water "ALL DAY," I saw my own water bottle in my purse.

As the teacher shut Emily's door, I rolled down the window and handed mine to the teacher. The teacher and I made eye contact and we both smiled. My water bottle had giant letters that read, "There may be wine in here."

~ Maggie

Still Alice

I was finishing up paperwork at school (I'm a teacher) when my phone rang. It was my friend Ann, from our book club. She asked "Did you remember that you have book club tonight?" I replied, "Yes, I knew we had book club." The book we were discussing at that night's meeting, *Still Alice*, was about a middle-aged woman diagnosed with Alzheimer's disease who was getting dates and times confused. I added "Yes, I'm coming, where is it?"

Ann paused and said, "It's at YOUR house. Ten women are in your driveway, waiting!" I had agreed to host the meeting months ago and had even RSVP'd to my own book club, without checking the address. Ann rallied the whole crowd to go back home, grab a bottle of wine and a snack, and head to her house. Five years later, they continue to call me "Still Alice".

~ V. Z.

Who Is This?
When I had identical twin girls, the sweet nurse cut the identification tags off the girls before we left the hospital. By the time I got home, I had forgotten which baby was which, but a return visit to the hospital for a blood test confirmed who was whom.

After that, my aunt bought monogrammed gold bracelets for each girl so we could tell them apart - which worked until the girls began to teethe, and they chewed off the bracelet clasps. We headed back to the hospital for another blood test. Within a few months, one of the girls developed a distinct birthmark on her stomach, but it was a long time before we did not have to check bellies to know our own children apart.

~ Lynn Shivers

9 TO 5ish
WOES AT WORK

When you fail at something,
you could try again and succeed.
OR, it could be the universe saying,
'This is not for you, so move it along.'
~ Amy Lyle

I Can See Your Business

I'm a yoga instructor and was bragging about my expensive new yoga pants to everyone in summer solstice class until I bent over in a downward-dog pose and a woman informed me that I had a hole in my pants and a string was hanging out.

Still in position, I asked, "The tag?" She shook her head "No" and whispered, "Tampon string."
~ E. Baxter

I'm Sick of Everything

One morning, I left my boss a voicemail, telling him I could not come into the office. I said I was very sick and probably contagious and needed to rest. I really poured it on thick, fake-sneezing and coughing the entire call. My boss was out on a weeklong business trip, so I thought he might not even realize that I was ever gone.

When he returned and didn't say anything on Monday or Tuesday, I thought I was in the clear. On Wednesday, though, he called me into his office and played my message, which sounded even more convincing than I had thought.

When the message ended, I simply said, "I'm a lot better now," and stood up to leave.

He put his finger in the air as a "hold on a minute" sign

because the message was still playing. After a three-second pause, I heard myself singing "Bohemian Rhapsody" at the top of my lungs, stopping only to order three tacos from Taco Bell. I'm not sure how long I recorded myself singing, but my boss finally cut it off after I belted out five "Galileos" in a row.

I closed my eyes and cringed, waiting for him to fire me, but he told me to go back to my desk. As I left, I swear he had a slight smile.
    ~ Thomas M.

We Are Not Communicating Well

Twenty people gathered in the boardroom to give one last pitch to our largest client. They had been loyal to our software for over a decade but had hired a new chief technology officer that was leaning toward a new vendor.

I had a new boss as well. Although he had been with the company for only a few months, he had an uncanny knowledge of what made people tick in our office. He walked me through my direct reports, sharing who he thought was more motivated by recognition than money, who he thought was shopping for another job, and who was most likely to get promoted. I told him I thought he was right on the mark and asked how he figured everyone out so quickly. He told me he was an expert listener and could read people's nonverbal cues, including their body language.

Our client's new CTO was a tiny, nervous, sweaty man. He would ask us a question, we would address it beautifully, and then he would shuffle in his seat and ask us the same question in a slightly different way. We seemed to be getting nowhere. My boss's administrative assistant stood up in the middle of the meeting and handed me a note from my boss, written in cursive, that said, "Match his body language."

I was seated directly across from the sweaty CTO and started to mimic everything he did. If he leaned back, I leaned back; if he ran his fingers through his hair or bit his lip, I did the same. When I looked down with raised eyebrows, as if to say, "See, I'm doing it!" my boss looked confused and exasperated.

Regardless of how we overcame the CTO's objections and how I matched his body language, the meeting ended. It didn't work; they were moving forward with another vendor. Everyone left the room except for me and my boss.

I was putting papers in my bag when he asked, "What the hell were you doing?" I told him it sounded like the CTO had a long history with the other vendor. My boss said, "Not that, why were you mocking him, copying his every move?"

I held up his note. "You told me to match his body

language." My boss let out a huge sigh and said softly, with his teeth clenched, "It said to WATCH his body language."

I replied, "That makes so much more sense."
~ Mike C.

The Days Run Together

I was a nanny to twins for an affluent family. The mother, Trish, wanted the girls dressed in the signature nova check of Burberry or at minimum decked out in Janie and Jack with Prada Mary Janes for preschool.

When I brought the kids down in cowgirl outfits, Trish was not happy. I pulled a folded flyer out of one of the girl's backpacks and explained it was Western Day. I reminded her she had to pick up the girls because I had a dentist appointment to replace a crown, but I would be home in time to start dinner.

By five, I was in their kitchen when Trish told me she had finally settled the kids down. They had been upset. When I asked why, she handed me the flyer that I had given her earlier in the day. "What?" I asked, as it clearly was an invitation for the kids to come in hats and boots to celebrate "Western Wednesday," and the kids had been so excited to wear their outfits.

She took a breath and said, "The other children were not wearing western outfits." I jumped in with, "Oh, because all of these stuck-up moms cannot let their children dress like children for one day. They must compete against one another in kiddy couture. That is bullshit..." I went on and on, but Trish interrupted me. "No. It's because it was Western Wednesday and today is Tuesday," she explained. I said, "Oh. Well," I said, "they can wear them again tomorrow," and went about my business.

~ Missy Bolt

That Hurts

My team was called into a meeting to be introduced to the new regional manager, and people were asked to stand up one by one around the room to describe their role and goals. When it was my turn, and I tried to stand up, I caught the unrolling hem of my pants with my high heel and it snapped me down like a rubber band, onto the table, head-first. I pretended like I was fine, but had a huge bruise by lunchtime.

~ Becky Robinson

Stop Staring

After landing a job with a huge law firm in Annapolis, I was celebrating with friends at a local pub. After a few drinks, I whispered to the table, "Don't look now, but there's a woman that looks exactly like me over there, and she won't stop staring at me."

My friend whispered back, "That's you. It's a mirror, Amy."

~ Amy Hall Pickard

This Takes the Cake

After working all sorts of jobs out of college – including as a graphic designer for a magazine and a stewardess on a yacht – I was finally able to attend Wilton Cake School and start my own business. I had been making hundreds of traditional one-layer cakes and was excited when a new client wanted an elaborate, multilayered creation for her mother's surprise fiftieth birthday party.

I worked for days on the client requested custom fondant designs, including a Macy's shopping bag, lipstick case, and a pair of purple high-heeled shoes. I packaged the fondant designs separately so that I could place each item on a different layer of the cake once I arrived at the event. My daughter, Savannah, and I carefully loaded the very tall, three-layered cake in my minivan trunk and headed to the venue.

Traffic was horrible, and I started to sweat. I wanted the cake to be completely set up before any of the guests arrived. As I was about to pull over to study the directions, my daughter pointed out the window. "Isn't that the club, Mom?" I had driven right past the location. I made a U-turn as soon as I could and hopped out of the van to unload the cake. When I opened the trunk, it looked like an explosion. Two of the three layers were completely destroyed, but the top level looked salvageable.

I set up the remaining layer, placed the fondant pieces

around it, and stuck a candle in the top. "Where are the other layers?" the client asked. I replied, "The truth is, they exploded in my trunk during my 180 on Peachtree Parkway, I'm so sorry, I will give you a huge discount." The client looked at the one-layer cake and then to me and said. "Alrighty. The show must go on."

Shortly after this incident, I closed the custom cake company. I changed to cake blogging, which does not require any transporting and I get to eat whatever I make.

~ Lise Ode
MomLovesBaking.com

The Kickback that Kicked-Back, Hard

I work in a coffee shop and am the oldest employee by twenty years. Since I started five months ago, my boss, Chip, had been asking all the employees to do a "kickback" at his place, which is what twenty-year-olds call hanging out. It's a small gathering of a group of friends, more than a get-together but less than a party.

Anyway, we were "kicking back" in the living room when Chip brought out a bong. I was surprised when all the employees gathered around to partake.

The combination of my coworkers razzing me about not fitting in, several wine spritzers, and the fact that I'm a forty-five-year-old woman with three little kids and two dogs who's working at the coffee shop because my husband left me for his administrative assistant, Teri, prompted me to take a few hits. At first, I felt really good and actually started to appreciate these young kids who were out in the world, trying to make their mark. But within a few minutes, when I tried to stand, I fell into the arms of Tiffany, the sweetest girl from the coffee shop.

I kept telling her I was sorry and wiping her hair with my hands because I had spilled my wine spritzer all over both of us. My boss noticed and helped me outside onto what looked like (or could have been) a refurbished 1950s-style glider. He sat me down and told me he'd be back in a few minutes.

He never returned and I woke up to the sounds of cars honking, my legs hanging over the end of the glider and a cat licking my hand, still sticky from the wine. I rushed home, showered, checked on my kids via text to the ex-husband (they were at his house for the weekend), and made it in for my shift at 10:00 a.m. I was absolutely exhausted and counting down the hours until I could crawl into bed.

No one asked anything about me getting high, falling on Tiffany, or even sleeping outside on patio furniture. The only thing they wanted to know was if I wanted to do another kickback that night. Ahh, to be young again.
    ~ T.S.

Hot in Cleveland

I work on a safety team for a giant organization that has manufacturing plants all over the country. Our Cleveland, Ohio, facility had been experiencing a few issues, and over the past few months, I was sent several times to get them moving in the right direction. I opened my email to see that my boss and other executives would be attending the next meeting in Ohio.

I was trying to get promoted and was excited for him to see firsthand the improvements that had been made in Cleveland. I was pushing him, in emails, about the initiatives that had been implemented and their positive impact on turnover, etc. I was lobbying for more responsibility.

I flew to Cleveland and arrived at the plant a little early, surprised that neither a coffee service nor breakfast had been set up in the executive boardroom, as a few of the higher-ups were coming in to talk about the next quarter's goals. I phoned one of the administrative assistants and asked why the room wasn't set up. She apologized and said she did not see the meeting on the calendar, but she could get everything in place within the hour. The meeting was supposed to start at 9:00 a.m., but luckily people were running late. Soon, the food arrived and documents that needed to be printed were perfectly lined up in front of each chair.

At 10:00 a.m., my boss had not arrived, and the plant

higher-ups were getting antsy to return to work. At 10:30, the administrative assistant told me I had a phone call.

I answered using the speaker phone and my boss asked where I was. I told him I was in the executive board room. He asked me "where exactly in the executive board room?"

I said, "The second floor, with the managers, what do you mean 'where'?"

He replied, "What city are you in?"

I laughed and said, "Cleveland, what city are you in?"

He did not laugh and said, "Columbus." Everyone in the room threw up their hands and headed back to work.

I had read over the meeting details so quickly that, when I saw "Ohio," I assumed Cleveland. I ran to my rental car and drove to Columbus. I was not promoted for another year.
   ~ Lance

That's Why They Call It Work

When I was thirty, I landed a paid-writing position in my hometown newspaper as a columnist. I didn't want anyone to know I was the author, so when the paper sent a photographer over to snap my picture for the announcement, I wore a blond wig. The photographer told me how to pose and at one point I was leaning over a wooden sign bearing the name of the cottage I lived in, *Florencia DeVille*.

As I was leaning over, I noticed my shirt had slipped down and my breasts were a little exposed. "Stop," I said. "Don't take any more pictures until I fix my blouse. I don't want all of England seeing my clitoris." The photographer stopped cold, then fell over laughing, and I laughed so hard I couldn't say "cleavage," which was what I meant. We both had to catch our breath and I had to reapply my makeup before we could continue.

~ Caroline Sherouse
Author, *Blow Me Over with a Feather*

Attention Kmart shoppers

When I was in high school, my friends and I were delinquents. We would peruse our neighbors' garage refrigerators for beer, and we'd smoke weed and skip school as much as possible. We wanted to up our up-to-no-good-game. We devised a plot to shoplift CDs from Kmart because we were too cheap to buy them, and we figured we could trade them for drugs. I could only talk one of my friends, Mark, into the scheme. I worked at Kmart, so I knew when the store was most-crowded. Also, I was buddies with some of the cashiers, and I could identify all of the security guards. Our plan should go off without a hitch. Everybody at Kmart liked me. To them, I was the tall, skinny, clean cut high school athlete that had overcome a disability. I was born with the congenital hand deformity symbrachydactyly; the underdevelopment of one's forearm and hands. I had tiny fingers on my right hand.

Mark and I had never shoplifted before and went on a practice run. We hit Fay's Drugstore because normally Fay was the only person in the store and could be easily distracted. We shoved bags of Goo Goo Clusters, Circus Peanuts, and candy corn down our pants and walked out the door. With the drugstore job completed without a hitch, we now had the confidence to take down Kmart.

We entered the store individually, so we wouldn't call attention to ourselves. I pretended to have a shopping list from my mother. Mark and I met up in the CD section and quickly sought out our assigned merchandise lifts. I was in charge of getting Mötley Crüe's "Dr. Feelgood", Alice Cooper's "Trash" and Metallica's "...And Justice for All". Since I had my roomy MC Hammer pants on, I also shoved the new "Batman" soundtrack by Prince and "Like a Prayer" by Madonna, which would get me points with my lady friend. Mark gave me the signal (three blinks with both eyes) that his mission had been completed as well.

As we were leaving the CD department, we noticed a security guard. I headed to the cashier and Mark followed. We both bought one CD and some gum to throw off any theft suspicion and left the store. We exited the Kmart and dumped our stash into my car.

From out of nowhere, a middle-aged security guard appeared, holding a badge and saying, "Hold it, boys, security."

Mark and I looked at each other and ran. We were varsity soccer players and lightning fast. We headed straight out of the parking lot, toward the road.

The security guard was screaming, "I'll get you punks!"

We lost the security guard and walked to a convenience store to call our friends, Richie and John. They picked us up and we hung out for a few hours at Burger King, until the Kmart closed. Just to be safe, Mark and I went to Richie's house while Richie and John went to pick up my car.

They drove the truck out of the Kmart parking lot without issue, only to be surrounded by police cars as soon as they were on the city street. It didn't take long for them to find Mark and I, pretending to be asleep at Richie's house. We were taken to the police station to be booked. After taking our mug shots they started the fingerprinting process. They were having a hard time getting prints from my tiny fingers; they kept putting my hand in the ink and trying to press it to the sheet. Scott asked, "So how did you guys know it was me?" The police officer replied dryly, "We were looking for a tall, skinny kid with a small right hand."

We were happy to spend the night in jail, as we knew we

would be in indescribable trouble with our parents once we were released.

~ Scott Specker and his Buffalo Posse

I May Get Violent

I was replying to my demanding boss via email that I was headed his way with the stacks of printed materials he needed for an important stockholders' meeting when I asked my coworker in the next cubicle over, "Did you print the files?"

I stopped typing for a second and heard, clip, clip, clip. I stood up to look over the wall to see his work shoes and black socks on his desk, he was hunched over the trash can, clipping his toenails. There were a thousand pieces of paper on his desk that still needed to be organized.

~ Anonymous

The Heavyweight Champion

When I was twenty and serving in the United States Navy, I gravitated toward three guys with similar priorities, such as the pursuit of lady friends and WWE. When we secured a WWE Heavyweight Championship belt replica, we all hung it around our shoulders and our waists and did our best Rock and Hulk Hogan impressions. Soon the belt became a trophy. You had to be worthy of the belt to wear it or even hold it. Rules were laid out.

1. Whoever holds the belt is the champion and must

retain it day and night.

2. Holding the belt means you can be challenged for the belt at any time.
3. The belt can only be won by pin, submission, or in rare cases being tossed from the designated wrestling area, aka Last Man Standing.

With these three rules in place, chaos ensued. Whoever held the belt was attacked on the ship: in your rack (bed), mess deck (dining room on a ship), or hallways; and, on land: in a park, in your car, or even on a date. Eventually a "Royal Rumble" of sorts was set up with submission, pin, and designated toss areas outlined.

Our antics had led us to take the battles underground, as we had been forbidden to engage in such roughhousing while on a naval ship. Nevertheless, we moved forward with the match, and all four of us entered the locked room aboard the Navy Guided Missile Destroyer.

Eight minutes into an intense battle, the coveted belt was within my grasp until I was thrown headfirst into a large metal cabinet. Undeterred, I turned to fight, but everyone had stopped and was staring wide-eyed, mouths agape. No one said anything. Blood dripped down my face as I mumbled taunting words to my opponent and then … collapsed. I was carried to the medical deck where I was asked what had happened.

I explained "the accident": a metal cabinet was open when I arose, and I cut my head. My wound required twenty stitches and two days of observation. The match had been postponed until another day, the title indefinitely on hold. I never was able to win the trophy, but when I shave my head, a scar runs from the front to the back, reminding me of the time I almost had a Heavyweight Championship belt.

~ James Creviston
The Clean Comedy Hour Podcast

So, No Tip?

I worked as a valet for Samuel's Grande Manor, an event venue for weddings, charity events and corporate parties. The event was in full swing and only a few cars were arriving, so our valet team had some extra time.

When a Toyota Supra pulled up, I opened the door. A huge man stepped out and told me the car was brand-new and to park it somewhere in the back where it would not be scratched. He was very cocky, acting like his Supra was a Bugatti.

I got into the car and put it in first gear, surprised by how great the engine sounded. I pulled around back to park it, but when I saw no other customers needed my attention, I opted to put the Supra to the test. A short strip of road ran behind the event building, so I peeled out, got it up to 100 mph, and then slammed on the brakes. It was so fun,

I did it three more times before parking the car.

When I walked back to put the keys in the cabinet, the Supra guy was waiting for me. "What the f*** were you doing? I saw you driving my car! I'm going to kill you!"

As I was racing the Supra back and forth on the strip, I had forgotten that the tables overlooking the backyard had a full view of the road.

~ Scott Williams

Keep Pulling

After months of asking Angie, my wife, to host a dinner for the executives of my company, she finally agreed. The CEO, Gary, and the COO, Walt, and their wives would join us for dinner.

Angie admittedly goes off the rails when company is expected. She rearranged the furniture several times, had the carpets steam cleaned, and for this dinner, scrubbed the air recirculation vent with a toothbrush. We also discussed our yellow Labrador named Stu. I wanted him to be left outside, but my wife preferred he stay inside, but out of the way. We decided to sequester him in our bedroom.

Halfway through the second course (roasted butternut squash and shallots), Gary and Walt said it was time to share some good news, but they paused when they heard Stu, barking and scratching on the door of the spare bedroom.

Gary said, "You have a dog? I love dogs! Bring him out!" Angie explained that he was a boisterous Lab and maybe we should wait until dessert to release him.

Walt threw in, "Don't be ridiculous! Let's see him!"

My wife excused herself from the table and retrieved Stu, who was delighted to be the center of Gary's and Walt's attention. He ran back and forth for what seemed like an hour. Finally, Stu settled down, lying half under the table by Gary, and we all enjoyed the rest of the meal.

Gary was in the middle of a serious discussion about the company making an acquisition and hinting that I might be up for a promotion when he looked down and picked up something from the floor. "Oh no," was all he said as he looked to me for help.

Stu had eaten a pair of Angie's pantyhose. He must have gone to the bathroom and a piece of it was still hanging from his butt. I grabbed a roll of paper towels and gently pulled. The nylon hose came out like a magician's scarf trick, like a never-ending stream of hosiery coming out of Stu's bottom. I kept tugging while everyone in the room stared—disgusted, yet mesmerized as one leg came out, then the crotch part of the hose, and finally the other leg, down to the toes.

"Dessert?" Angie practically cried, not knowing what to do.

They shook their heads and mumbled a soft, "No, thank you." We retrieved their coats and the night was over.

I did eventually get a promotion but my boss has never let me live down the pantyhose-dinner. He does an exaggerated reenactment of the event, pretending to pull out what seemed like a hundred yards of pantyhose from our Labrador retriever's butt, every chance he gets.
~ A.S.

Editors' Note: Never pull anything out of your animal's bottom, you could hurt them. Call your veterinarian.

We're Not That Close

I was at a conference in Utah for essential oils with a good friend. We were so happy to be rooming together because we were both self-proclaimed germaphobes. My bare feet have never touched the floor of a hotel and Jen brought her own TravelFresh Sleepsack so her body would not touch the hotel sheets.

The conference was going great until Jen and I were getting ready for dinner and she gave me the most horrifying look as I was brushing my tongue. She looked at me and then to my toiletries bag on the shelf beneath the sink. I stepped back while gesturing, "What?" with a mouthful of toothpaste. It was then that I saw MY toothbrush sticking out of my toiletries bag. Mine was the exact same make and model as hers. I had been using the wrong toothbrush for three days straight. I bought her a new one from the hotel and neither of us ever spoke of it again.

~ Jodi Dow Christensen

I Can Take You Home, Sir

While in college, I was parking cars for a country club that hosted all sorts of events at night when the golf club was closed, such as weddings and Christmas parties. We stored all the keys in a steel cabinet. People would often lose their valet tickets or hand me the ticket and then point to their keys, saving me from matching up the numbers. I appreciated their help, as the faster I retrieved the cars and the more customers I helped meant the more money I would make in tips.

One night, I had been working a large wedding and people started to pour out, wanting their cars. At the end of the night, only five key sets remained when a gentleman came out and was looking in his pockets for his ticket. I asked if he knew which keys were his and he said "Yes", pointing to a set of keys on an almost Slinky-style bracelet. (I remember swinging the stretchy bracelet around as I ran to get his Buick.) He gave me twenty dollars—the biggest tip of the night—and told me I was a good kid.

An hour later, the father of the groom came out and handed me his ticket, which did not match any of the keys. I asked him if he saw his keys hanging in the cabinet. He said no, but his keychain looked like a black Slinky bracelet and he drove a Buick. I told him I had already given those keys to a gentleman over an hour ago. We called the police, but they never found the car until it showed up several weeks later, in the exact same place I had parked it at the wedding. The car was completely trashed. The police said it was probably used in some sort of drug run. The club's insurance paid for the damages and initiated a, "No ticket, no car," policy after the incident.

~ Sam Moche

Excuse Me

I was meeting with several employees to discuss our law firm's dress code. We have clients in the office daily, so we asked the attorneys to wear suits and allow the staff to dress in business casual. In the employee handbook, we describe the style as less formal than traditional business suits, but still providing a professional impression. A few of the ladies in the office had thought the policy was just a suggestion and were starting at best, to look more like yoga instructors with athletic wear and at worse, like hookers wearing mini-skirts and tank-tops.

It was uncomfortable for me to be discussing employment issues with the staff because I'm the wife of the firm's founder and I normally only work on marketing materials and such. But the attorneys thought that discussing dress code violations with female employees would be better received from a woman. And they wanted the staff to see an example of business casual (I always wore slacks, a button-down shirt or a nice blouse and loafers).

My loafers made the meetings even more awkward. They were super snug at the top, so they kept making squishy fart noises as I walked. All day, everyone heard, "Parrp, parrp, parrp," as I made my way from one employee's office to the next. It's hard to stay confident and instruct people on how you need for them to improve their level of professionalism when your opening line is, "Hello, I'm not farting, it's my shoes."

~ K.B.

The Billionaire and the Texan

While going to college part-time, I worked full-time at a swanky golf club as the clubhouse manager. One of our wealthiest clients, a media mogul, had a private jet, and we were required to retrieve the billionaire and his party from the airport. We knew the drill. Because he never wore the same clothes twice, we provided fresh shirts and pants daily from the pro shop. We arranged for a professional to help him with his swing, and we made sure he had the tuna on toast points that he wanted for lunch.

On one particular trip, he brought a group of professional polo players who belonged to the team that he owned. We delivered everyone safely to their villas and we were scheduled to accommodate them in the morning for eighteen holes of golf. After an uneventful day of golf, the group was scheduled for dinner.

At some point, the mogul became disenchanted with the polo team and took off to Vegas without them, even though the team was expected to be there for a marketing event the next day. So we scrambled to book NetJets to pick them up. My boss instructed me and my coworker, Rob, to stay with them to make sure they got to the Bellagio, and then to the billionaire.

Rob and I checked into the hotel and were enjoying watching the mogul's impressive winning streak at the craps table when an "obnoxious Texan" (as he called him) showed up. Everything about the Texan was big—his hat, boots, belt buckle, but mostly, his mouth. He was a sore loser and a braggadocious winner, all while managing to insult the two ladies glued to his arm, the boxman, all the dealers, and anyone else within a ten-foot radius of him.

Rob and I were next to the mogul, who was growing wearier of the Texan by the second. After the Texan had bragged about the size of his cows and his penis, the mogul took a deep breath and calmly asked him, "Hey, Texas, what's your total net worth?"

The Texan beamed with pride and announced—not just to the mogul, but to the table, "Over one hundred million."

The mogul took a chip from his winnings and presented it to the Texan, saying, "I'll flip you for it." The Texan looked around and then back to the mogul, who asked again,

"Heads or tails for the hundred million?"

The mogul held the chip very close to the Texan, who, for once, was silent until he screamed, "That's some crazy shit!" He then threw out orders to a few people around him and the whole group left.

The mogul nodded at me and I knew Rob and I should move on. The next day, when Rob and I checked out, the front desk had an envelope for me. I knew what was in it. Every time the billionaire visited the golf club, he always left me the same gratuity: $10,000 in cash to be shared with the staff.

~ P.C.

And They Laughed and Laughed

My regular manicurist, Jan, was out when I went in to get a mani/pedi. I know I sounded so picky, explaining all the details of what I wanted, when I requested American-style nails (a paler version of French nails) from the new lady. "I don't care for pink pink, only pale pink. It has to look natural. Please don't make the white line too thick, and not too white—pale, like a real fingernail. I would like them squared off, not round or pointy." I went over a different set of instructions for my pedicure.

When she was finished (they looked great), we were moving to the drying station together and I apologized. "I'm so sorry. I know I sound really demanding. I have a huge appointment later today and everything has to be perfect. Jan has been doing my nails for years and she knows exactly what I want. I hope you understand. I'm not normally this finicky. I have a major meeting in a few hours."

The new lady understood only a fraction of what I was saying. The other ladies in the shop were talking to her and I think, judging by their facial expressions, they were telling her how difficult I was and how only Jan could handle me. I heard Jan's name several times. As I turned to sit at the drying station, the new lady grabbed my hand, not wanting me to sit down.

"What's happening?" I said, confused when she kneeled down and started attending to my pants. She pulled out a piece of toilet paper and kept pulling. It must have been three feet long. Everyone in the salon was looking at me. I was waving my still-wet nails in the air as she delicately kept pulling and neatly folding the toilet paper as she went. Finally, when it was all out, she laid the stack of toilet paper on the counter of the drying station.

"You sit, you dry and then you will be perfect," she said. The whole salon snickered.

~ Carolyn Callaway Watters

Please Be Seated

I worked at a swanky country club and was tasked with picking up a group of Wall Street big-wigs who had flown into the Don Scott airport in their private jet at 7:00 a.m. I had been out all night and was running late, so I grabbed the keys to the 15-person passenger van and raced out.

I made it just in time to meet eight businessmen dressed in suits, standing with their luggage and golf bags. I jumped out, grabbed one of their golf bags, and opened the back doors of the van. There were no seats. We frequently remove the seats, depending on what we needed to haul, and in my haste, I hadn't noticed.

The head Wall Streeter sat in the passenger seat and the other seven squatted on the metal floor while balancing their luggage and golf bags. My boss did not appreciate the situation. He vacillated- apologizing to the guests and yelling at me. The Wall-Streeters must have gotten a kick out of it, as they insisted on tipping me $200.
~ P.J.C.

Is That A Toenail in Your Soup?

I had nervously chewed my fingernails with the ferociousness of a rabid ferret until they resembled bloody stumps that mocked my lack of self-control. Scheduled for an important business meeting at an exclusive private club, I frantically searched through my drawers to find press-on fingernails, but all I could find were press-on toenails, which I had purchased by mistake. I was desperate, so I attached them to my ravaged fingers and dashed to the meeting.

Somewhere between the soup and salad, the nails began to pop off and tumble to the table until my plate was surrounded by fake toenails, and the pinky toenail was floating in my soup! My luncheon companions pretended not to notice, and I brushed the offensive, useless bits of plastic into my purse, folded my abused hands in my lap, smiled, and continued the business conversation.

~ Elaine Ambrose
Author, *Midlife Happy Hour*

Feeling Hot, Hot, Hot

When I was working as a flight attendant, I did not put the top of the coffee carafe on properly and dumped the steaming contents on a professional athlete's lap. All he said was, "Wow. That is very, very hot on my crotch area."

~ Andrea

That Really Stinks

I once worked with over one hundred accounting assistants, accountants and CPAs. One of the managers, Kevin, was unbelievably smart and generous as a boss. He had horrible allergies and was always sniffing and spoke as if he had a severe cold. He was notorious for coming into our cubicles, standing by us with a file, leaning over, and passing gas. His butt was literally at the height of our noses and he never said "excuse me" or left. Maybe he couldn't smell his own funk because he just stood there, telling us what to do, with both of us surrounded by the most horrific fart stench. The only time it was ever addressed was when another manager caught us giggling about it in the lunchroom. She screamed, "He has stomach problems!" "No kidding," we mumbled.

~ Contributed by Joy G.

I'm Feeling Slightly Woozy

It was 2006 and I was at Ft. Bragg in the Psychological Operations Battalion. Our lieutenant colonel was leaving and wanted one last hurrah, so we scheduled an Airborne jump (since we were an Airborne unit) out of Black Hawk helicopters. If you had your wings, you went on the jump. If you were air assault (rappelling out on ropes from the helicopter), then you did that. If you were neither (a "leg"), then you would take a seat on the Black Hawk. I was in charge of taking photos and video, until it was our turn.

We waited around all day, ate MREs (Meals Ready to Eat) and then hopped on the last Black Hawk of the four. The pilots were glad it was almost over and had a blast dipping and doing all kinds of tricks. I normally have a very strong stomach and love roller coasters, but something about this twenty-five-minute ride plus a bad MRE wasn't sitting right. So after about ten minutes, I knew I was going to be sick.

There are no motion-sickness bags in military aircrafts and I wasn't going to throw up on the floor. In desperation, I vomited right down my shirt. It was tucked in so the vomit pressed against my body. Once the pilots knew I'd gotten sick, they took the helicopter on even more daring dips.

Next, we had to jump out and pretend we were at war, lying down in the prone position. I was lying down in my own puke.

A few days later, we were at the rehearsal for the change of command and one of the leaders called me over and introduced me to the command sergeant major (basically the highest rank of the enlisted in my brigade). He said, "This is PFC Hicks."

"OH! You're the one who got sick yesterday."

With a beet-red face, I said, "Yes sir, Command Sergeant Major."

"Well," said the command sergeant major, "I have to say that you did the right thing. I had the same thing happen to me on my way to Afghanistan and had to retch into my helmet. It has to do with your inner ears. I'm proud of you for the quick thinking."

For the rest of my time in the service, if anyone threw up during a flight, they would tease them and say they had "Pulled a Hicks."
~ Erika Hicks

My Worst Day
My morning alarm went off on my cell phone, but my phone was in my purse, in my bathroom, in the closet, so I

didn't hear it and was running late for work. (I manage an art center where people can make different do-it-yourself projects, such as yard art, splatter painting, mugs—that sort of thing.) The day flew by. We had hosted three birthday parties for kids painting their own birdhouses, and two soon-to-be brides making cute wooden wedding signs with their bridesmaids. When I had a minute to think, I realized I was starving. One of my employees offered me half her protein shake that she had gotten from across the street during a party turnover. I asked her what it was, and she rattled off some sort of espresso concoction.

"Does it have any berries in it?" I asked. She took a sip and said she didn't think so and proceeded to pour some into a small cup for me. I chugged it and then detected a slight berry flavor. "I think this has berries in it. I'm terribly allergic to strawberries," I said.

I called my boyfriend to bring me an EpiPen. My throat was already starting to feel tight when Michael arrived with Benadryl. He handed me five small tablets, saying he had been out (not at home) and didn't have access to the EpiPen. I took the tablets and sipped some water. Just as I started to say that I felt better, I fell face forward, into a table of still-wet birdhouses, and then bounced to the floor, facedown.

Michael called 911 while a guest called poison control. The good news, she announced, was that five Benadryl pills would most likely NOT kill me. Meanwhile, the ambulance showed up and took me to the hospital while the ENT doctor called in the situation as an overdose. Several hours later, after receiving some fluids, I was released. It was after 10:00 p.m. by the time we got home, and I still had not eaten anything.

Sweet Michael said he would get my favorite snack, a Wild Naked Chicken Chalupa and several Cheesy Roll Ups from Taco Bell. Michael grabbed my keys on the way out because my car was parked behind his in our narrow driveway. I was feeling much better, eating my late dinner, snuggled up with Michael and watching an episode of *Game of Thrones*, when he broke the news that he had to take an Uber home because he crashed my car into the back of a pickup truck while telling my mother I had overdosed on Benadryl—she screamed so loudly he accidentally hit the gas rather than the brake in the drive-thru line at Taco Bell. The car was towed to a repair shop.

He said he didn't tell me earlier because it would have ruined my chalupa experience. We're getting married in the fall.

~ T.S.

Cover Your Buttons

My boss, Howard, the president of the bank, was very old school. We still had to wear skirts or dresses that hit our knees or below and closed-toed shoes, and our shoulders had to be covered. Only recently did he remove pantyhose from the dress-code requirements. When Marion, who had transferred to our branch from a Miami office, arrived for our Monday morning meeting in a silky dress with a jacket, but sans bra to support her giant, drooping breasts, I thought Howard was going to go into cardiac arrest on the spot. Howard insisted I join him so he could "address the knockers situation."

We went into Marian's office and sat in the two chairs across from her desk. Howard handed Marian the dress-code rules from the employment manual. He had highlighted the phrase "professional attire." When Marion responded as if she had no idea what he was referring to, Howard started rattling off what seemed to be every synonym for modest, including chaste, proper, discreet, and demure.

Marion went nuts. She stood up, removed her jacket and launched into how bras represented the oppression of all women and the history of unequal pay and opportunities, and that she would not go backwards out of respect for all the feminists that had fought for her. Marion sat down and looked to me with a look that said, "Can you believe this guy?"

I told Marion quietly, "Your breasts ARE very distracting to both men and women at the office. Maybe you could wear a tank top with some support?"

Marion took a deep breath and said, "For you, Joan, I will consider that option." She then jerked open her desk drawer, pulled out her cell phone, laid it on the desk, and then screamed, "I said I would consider it! Now leave my office!"

And she slammed the drawer shut on her large breasts.

Marion squealed, I jumped up to help her, and Howard left the office. For years, at company holiday parties after Howard had his third glass of scotch, he would remind me of the incident and defend his insistence on brassieres in the office. He always ended his rant with, "It's a damn safety issue."

~ Joan S.

Pardon Me

I was attending a literary event focused on writing "the truth," and I was wearing a gorgeous evening gown. The setting was amazing, so I was taking a few photos when a group asked if I could take a few shots of them in front of an incredible water feature. I agreed, and a woman handed me her camera. They all gathered together, and I took the photograph and showed them. They asked if I could take another one, with an upward angle that showed the fountain in the shot.

I went down a few steps and crouched awkwardly on the floor in my evening gown. It seemed very quiet and then

… I farted, really loudly. It seemed like it lasted for five seconds, just a nonstop fart. It was like I was in someone else's body.

I said, "Oh my goodness, I'm so sorry." The group mumbled that they hadn't heard anything and scattered. I even had to chase down the lady to return her camera. I was mortified, but oddly inspired to write about it, as the whole focus of the seminar was to be real. A squatty fart in a gown in front of complete strangers is about as truthful as it gets.

~ "Barb" (Too embarrassed to use her real name)

Let Me Introduce You

After graduating from college, I worked temp positions for almost a year while trying to find a "real job." One Friday, as I was tidying up the front desk where I had been working as a receptionist on and off, the president of the company, Mr. Newman, paused before he left for the weekend. He asked me if I would want to be brought on permanently as a receptionist. I thanked him, but shared that I was a graphic artist and was willing to do design work for the same wage as the receptionist job to gain some experience.

Mr. Newman asked what my level of interest was in technology, as the firm sold some sort of technology and needed some marketing assistance in that department. I lied and said I was very interested, even though, other than my graphic design work on a Mac, I had zero experience or interest in technology. I'm a fast learner, though, and I knew if they gave me the opportunity, I would rise to the occasion.

By the end of the following week, the temp company and the technology company had come to an agreement and I was offered a full-time job in a graphic-design role with better wages, full benefits and two weeks' vacation. Mr. Newman asked if I could join a call Thursday night with the American and London marketing departments, which was the group I was supporting. Because London is five hours ahead of us, the call started at 11:00 p.m.

Mr. Newman gave me strict instructions. "Listen carefully to the call, but don't say anything. I may introduce you at the end." He paused and added, "Put your computer on mute. We don't need any distractions."

At 11:00 p.m., I entered the conference-call code that was provided to me into my new, company-provided laptop and waited. A few seconds went by and then I could see a conference room where a well-dressed woman was going through a file frantically and saying, "Blast it!" as if she forgot to print something. Within seconds, several people piled into the room and around the table. There was a lot of chatter.

I hit the mute button but wanted to test it, so I yelled into my computer, "Hello! Hello! I can see you. Can you see me?" No reply. I sat the laptop on my coffee table and settled in with a cup of tea and listened.

The meeting had been going on for ninety minutes and I did not understand a word they were saying about global market share and shifting platforms, but I was taking notes. After three cups of tea, I really had to use the bathroom, so I carried the laptop into the powder room, set it next to me on the small chest of drawers that held toilet paper, and pulled down my pants to go. I relieved myself, wiped and flushed.

The people in the room stopped cold. They started looking at each other. I pulled up my pants and watched, but no one moved. They looked as if they were waiting for something to happen as well.

Finally, the woman that I had first seen when I logged in looked straight at the screen and said, "We can see you."

As I slowly closed the laptop, I heard my boss telling the team, "That's Kelly. She'll be doing your marketing."
    ~ Kelly B.

Extra Marinara

While a student at Auburn University, after serving time in an ice-cream shop and a fast-food joint, I was finally making great (college) money working in a swanky Italian restaurant. A few guests even asked for me by name. My favorites were an older couple that always updated me on their handsome son, Mario, who was finishing up his cardiology residency in Chicago. They went on and on about Mario being the smartest, most handsome boy in the world and they wanted him to "meet a nice girl like YOU." They always came on "'Tini Tuesdays" to get our featured half-price martinis. Rita, the wife, always ordered a Gibson and Hal would get his "very dry."

One night, they requested a table for three because their son was in town. Hal wanted his usual, the lasagna; Rita, the caprese salad, because Hal "could never finish his dinner" and she "didn't like the waste." They added the veal parmesan for their son, who would be arriving any minute. Rita said, "He would like extra marinara," but Hal clarified, "Swimming in marinara, pour it on the top and add a bowl on the side. We'll pay the extra—he loves marinara."

As I approached their table with their dinners, the bartender caught my attention and placed another round on my tray AND I caught the eye of Mario, the extra-marinara, soon-to-be-cardiologist. He was strikingly handsome. I must have lowered my tray by just an inch as I swung around because my elbow caught the tip of the bar, making me project the entire tray of food toward Rita, Hal and Mario with the velocity of (Hall-of-Fame pitcher) Greg Maddux. The crash of the glasses, plates and tray was deafening. I looked down at the mess for just a second before coming eye to eye with Hal, who looked like a stabbing victim— he had marinara sauce dripping down his face. I was speechless, while the other waiters and manager rushed in to help wipe everyone down, saying, "We'll pay for everything—the meal, your next meals, the dry cleaning ..."

I cried, feeling so badly about the mess. When Rita approached me, I thought she would give me some words of wisdom or at least tell me it was okay. Instead, she just told me she wanted her order to go. I never saw them again.
~ Shannon Krogman, Yoga Instructor

Everybody's Shufflin'
Straight out of college, I headed to a mid-sized computer-brokerage firm to do administrative work. We were a hardware chop-shop, buying huge lots of used computers, tearing them apart and reselling them. Europe was a major market for us, as their technology trailed the United States.

Kari was hired in sales support at the same time I was. Fluent in several languages, she was ecstatic to land a job requiring the use of her fluent Spanish, Italian and German. Often, she would have to put the interested party on hold to walk back to the warehouse to eyeball a piece of equipment if a tech was not picking up her call. Because of the way she walked, the entire company— about three hundred people—called Kari "the Shuffler."

Kari prided herself on her secondhand-store finds before vintage was cool. Most days she smelled like mothballs or cigarettes because she was too thrifty to waste quarters to launder her new/old digs. She would have looked super groovy in her flared polyester trousers and Peter Pan collars if they would have been the right size, but she was driven by price more than fashion or fit. All day long, from the sales floor to the warehouse to the lunch room, and to the fax machine, we could hear her shuffling.

Dan, her boss, was appalled when he saw her shuffling. "Pick up your damn feet!" he screamed as she shuffled from the office supply room to the lobby where he was waiting. She shuffled faster. He told her again when she was next to him, "It's annoying to the entire office that you don't pick up your feet. WHY don't you pick up your feet?"

"I have really small feet, and buy all my shoes at secondhand stores, so they would fall off if I lifted my feet," she replied. She lifted up one foot, and her shoe dropped to the floor.

We couldn't hear what he said to her next, as he lowered his voice to a whisper, but he must have read her the riot act or given her a raise to buy new shoes because from that day forward, she never shuffled again.

~ A.L.

Strange Attachments

I was only one of hundreds churning out reports for a giant organization. My cubicle was the last in a row of at least fifty others. The only time I got a glimpse of real light was when Carol, the executive secretary to the president, Mr. Kaufmann, would open the door of her office to run down the hall to grab a report or pick up the catering delivery. Surrounded by the sounds of keyboards clicking, cell phones dinging, and my coworkers' gum smacking, I dreamed of an office with natural light and a door.

It was a Tuesday when I noticed the executive secretary's office was dark. When I investigated, I found it abandoned and spotless. I was running my fingers over the large desk when Mr. Kaufmann came in, asked for my name, and then sadly explained that Carol, his favorite assistant of twenty years, was having a family emergency in Schenectady. He said he would never find someone else who worked as diligently as she did.

I told him that I had started as a receptionist and then worked as a proofreader and then a manager and would love the opportunity to be his assistant. After a few questions about my computer skills and event-planning experience, I was hired.

Mr. Kaufmann, who was over seventy, was a wonderful boss whom I rarely saw. He'd email me requests and I'd drop the printed reports in his inbox. One day I was surprised to see him standing in my doorway, waving travel documents around. He was booked to Chicago, but there was a fiasco brewing in San Diego; he asked if I could please redo all the arrangements. He sat down next to me as I pulled up the company travel software. "I'll wait," he said.

As I turned to get his itinerary off the printer, I noticed a large black hair across his face. "I'm so sorry, Mr. Kaufmann. One of my hairs must have landed on your face," I said. He swatted at it to no avail. I said, "I'll get it," and delicately tried to brush it off. The hair resisted. It was attached to his nose. "Hold on," I said, as I got a firmer grip and yanked it out.

He cringed for a second and his eyes filled up with tears. "Thank you, Anna," he whispered. He grabbed his itinerary off the printer and left my office. I worked for him for a decade and we never again spoke of the incident.
    ~ Anna Sander

It Will All Work Out

I was working as the sales manager for a large sales team. Monthly, about thirty people came into the office to go over new products, forecasts and such. An additional fifty people would join us remotely via conference call. The company had been growing like crazy and I was delighted when our president, Martin, wanted to join the call to give a few congratulatory shout-outs to a few top performers.

Just as I had wrapped up some forecasting details for our group and was getting ready to introduce him, we heard, "Sheila, please, I know you're there. Call me back."

I was in the conference room with about twenty regional

salespeople and Martin. We awkwardly looked at one another and then Martin cleared his throat to make his statements just before we all heard, "Shelia, baby, I was wrong. You told me NOT to go with Hector, and just so you know, it was his idea to get the burner phones. I did not have sex with any of them. They were ESCORTS, not hookers. You have to believe me."

Martin asked me who was on the phone. I shrugged my shoulders, not knowing anything about an employee involved with a Sheila or a Hector. We were interrupted again when the mysterious salesperson continued his one-way plea. "Sheila, it's me, Hugh. The same Hugh that loves to rub your back every night, that loves *When Harry Met Sally*–"

"HUGH!" Martin said. There was a pause but no reply. Martin went back to business, saying, "We all have challenges, some more than others, like our brother Hugh, but we must overcome them …"

Hugh and Sheila eventually worked things out, got married and had twin girls. Our entire sales force knew the updates because invariably on our monthly sales calls an employee would ask, "Hugh, how's Sheila?"
　　~ C.T.W.

The Party Is Over
Once out of college, I was ready to rock the world with my health promotion degree from the University of Georgia.

144

After sending out hundreds of resumes and getting few responses (beyond "Don't call us, we'll call you" from the handful of interviews I managed to secure), one of my roommates pulled some strings and helped me land a job as an event coordinator with a corporate event-planning firm called Fun Times.

They offered themes such as "Western," which featured pony rides and barbecues to "Circus", which featured clowns and funnel cakes. Their office was in an old, industrial part of Atlanta, and next to the event-planning building was an enormous, blocks-long distribution center where hundreds of 18-wheelers constantly pulled in and out. On the corner were prostitutes soliciting the truck drivers.

The job description said I would be responsible for the safety of the guests and for displaying food in an attractive manner, as well as other miscellaneous tasks. I was also required to secure a commercial driver's license because I would be driving the party equipment to the locations.

For my first event, I traveled across the country, sitting shotgun in an 18-wheeler to another recent college graduate. We arrived in Indiana on the hottest day in July to coordinate a midday picnic for a large world organization that promoted children's safety in the home. The client's human resources team greeted us on site and gave us instructions about what they wanted for their "Kids' Wonderland" event. They were particular about everything

– the location of the petting zoo, jumpy house, and the hot dogs and cotton candy stands, as well as which of our staff would greet the guests. We also had a ten-minute discussion about where the drinks would go. We normally set up drink machines with ice so people could serve themselves, but the client insisted we fill over two hundred glasses with soft drinks, tea, and lemonade before the guests arrived because it was so hot and they didn't want a line.

Less than thirty minutes into the event, we lost a family of five to the urgent-care clinic because their toddler broke out in violent-looking hives from contact with either the miniature donkeys or the bunnies in the petting zoo. All of the guests were terribly hot and thirsty, but no one dared to get a drink because thousands of bees were hovering and foraging in the lemonade and soda cups. Two adults and one child had already been treated by the company nurse for stings. The whole crowd was alerted because one of the executive assistants would shriek, "Get some ice to stop the venom from spreading!" during each occurrence.

The final straw was my fault and mine alone. I was in charge of the giant, inflated jumpy house and had neglected to review the extensive checklist that was provided. Everything seemed to be going well until the generator made a sputtering sound and – just seconds later – the entire two-story house cascaded down on the jumpers inside. I had forgotten to check the generator's fuel level. In a panic, a parent called 911.

Despite my Fun Time peers instructing parents to wait as we rolled the tarps back to claim the scared and now extra-sweaty youngsters, they rushed the house, stepping on other people's children still under the tarp to retrieve their own kids. The EMTs treated:

- seven twisted ankles, from parents climbing in the deflated jumpy house
- two children after being stepped-on by a stranger while waiting to be rescued
- our own employee, Dale, who tried to run away from the swarm of wasps attacking his cotton candy station
- additional bee stings
- over ten cases of dehydration
- one broken wrist - exact cause unknown

I was fired for violating 157-E, "Inspect generator fuel levels," and moved on to real estate, but sometimes, I still hear the screams.

~ Angela W.

Editor's Note: No one was seriously injured.

Rapid Fire

When I worked for Lancôme, one of my coworkers, who worked for Clinique, would slide open the product case door, fart, then close the case door. Very unladylike. Made me laugh every time.

~ M. Walsh

So, You Will Not Be Buying a House?
I normally wash my car by hand because I'm persnickety, but as I was rushing to meet a potential buyer for a property I had listed, I ran my Toyota SUV through the drive-thru car wash.

After showing the clients the house, we walked to the driveway together. I ran my hand across my car and said, "Oh my gosh, those drive-thru car washes are the worst. My car is still filthy." I held up my dirty hand in disgust. "Just look at this," I said as I scrunched up my nose.

"That's OUR car," they replied in unison. I hadn't noticed that we had the exact same make and model. They didn't want to see any other listings.
    ~ Carolyn Waters

I Need A Little Rest
I used to work in a historic district. The bathroom had a clawfoot tub. My coworkers and I would often find Chuck, the janitor, sleeping in it.
    ~ Katie M

Prepare for Landing
When I was in my fifties, I wanted to be someone besides "Mrs. Thomas." I loved being a wife and raising four kids, but I needed something of my own. I applied for a flight-attendant position with a major airline and got the job. I began working with a crew on a DC, a smaller aircraft, and

there were only two attendants. I was working the back, while my partner, Ally (also fresh from training) handled the front. As fast as we could, we distributed drinks, snacks, blankets - whatever people wanted. I was putting on another pot of coffee when I looked out the window and saw trees. "Oh my God, I wish we weren't flying so low to the ground," I said out loud.

A passenger looked at me and the other attendant, who was still offering drinks to passengers, and said, "Dear, we're landing."

Within seconds, we touched down - the beverage cart rolling, coffee pots spilling - as the captain said, "Welcome to Atlanta!" Ally and I were so busy getting through the service we missed the message about securing the craft. Luckily, no one was hurt.

~ Marla K

Excuses, Excuses

I had a coworker who would offer the most ridiculous excuses for being late to work. Her two favorites were "My cat threw up" and "I'm locked in my garage and can't get out."

~ Sadia. R.

Lemon Fresh

I worked in an office with "Spritzer Woman." When she was in the loo doing her business, I'd suddenly hear the sound of air freshener being spritzed, but she was a stealthy creature. I never saw her come out of the stall or the restroom.

~ L. D.

I Should Have Inhaled

Early in my career, I was employed at a fast-growing company. Through acquisitions and partnerships, we had expanded to include several companies and over fifty offices. The CEO of my company had a scheduling conflict, so he asked me to stand-in for him at an internal planning and strategy conference with the other C-level executives from our sister companies. I was very excited, and I was thinking my father will be proud to hear about my trip and my engagement with these VIPs.

The event was in Washington, D.C., and we wrapped up the week with a dinner at the prestigious University Club. After dessert, "celebratory" cigars were passed around the table. I am not a regular cigar smoker, but I have had a few in the past. In between the stories and the laughter, a small piece of tobacco had found its way into the back of my mouth, and I tried to retrieve it as discretely as I could. Somewhere between my continuing to puff and my oral gyrations, I swallowed a gullet full of smoke - not inhaled - but swallowed.

I began to cough as quietly as I could, but I could tell this wasn't going to end well. I recovered enough to finish most of the cigar, and then it was time to leave. I continued my recovery efforts while the valet retrieved our rented passenger van to take us back to our hotel. While we were waiting for the van, the bottom dropped out of the sky and the rain began to pour.

As we climbed into the van, I realized it would be best if I sat next to the door. As I began to shut the sliding door, the smoke in my stomach sought its release, along with my dinner. The good news is, I was able to deposit about half of the contents outside the van. The bad news is the other half wanted to go along for the ride.

Naturally, with the hard rain coming down, the best the other passengers could do was to roll down the windows a half-inch, as they sought some desperately-needed fresh air. In the silent and awkward ride back to our hotel, I found some solace from the situation in knowing my dad would be spared any knowledge of this particular trip.

~ Bobby Darnell
Author, *Time for Dervin*

Stinky Balls

My company's idea of holiday fun was Bingo. I was assigned to help with churning the bingo cage and selecting the numbers. The numbers looked as if they had been written on with a Sharpie.

As I was inspecting the bingo balls, my coworker bragged that he had made the set. Over the course of several years, he had painstakingly been removing the balls from his roll-on deodorant, washing them, and saving them in a pickle jar.

I moved to bingo-card verification.

~ B.M.

I Need To Watch My Stories

A guy brought a small TV to work so that he could watch talk shows and soap operas - no smartphone viewing with discreet headphones, a full-on TV with volume. And they never fired him.

~ Allison E

Misuse of the Facilities

My coworker, Kelly, was approaching maternity leave and we had been interviewing people for months to take over her spot during her twelve weeks off. Finally, Kelly and our boss unanimously agreed on a candidate, whom we would refer to as "New Mike."

"New Mike" started a few weeks before Kelly left so that he could get trained on her accounts, our new software system, and the company in general. When Katie left, New Mike stepped in seamlessly for the first four or five weeks, then he started missing deadlines and would be missing from his desk more and more often.

One day, while in line for a tuna roll-up in the building

deli, I overheard the guys in front of me making jokes about "Masturbation Mike." I interrupted them and asked what he looked like. They proceeded to describe our new hire, New Mike, and elaborated on how they were waiting for the one stall in the men's bathroom because the same guy was in there "taking care of another type of business." I told them I thought that was New Mike.

He was fired shortly after for not hitting deadlines, and forever after, "New Mike" was referred to as "Masturbation Mike" by all who knew him in the building.
    ~ Anonymous

Don't Touch That Dial!
There's a guy on my floor who scratches his man parts, then touches our shared radios.
    ~ Megan P

Who Are You Calling a B**ch?
In the mid-1990's, I was working for a small publishing company as one of only three people in the technology department. Since our boss was located in Europe, my co-worker, Tiger, and I had free reign to do nearly whatever we wanted - as long as we did our work.

The company was purchased by a Canadian company, and in the weeks that followed, a series of new work rules began to trickle into our previously rule-free world. Our new boss was a woman who lived in Toronto, and she was constantly sending emails to us regarding some new policy or procedure.

One afternoon, she sent us an email about new policy that was going to be a minor annoyance. I was a little miffed at this point, and I forwarded the email to my co-worker, and responded with, "Who does this b**ch think she is?"

In hindsight, the policy wasn't really that bad, and I was only looking to get a laugh out of my co-worker. And it would have worked, except I hadn't clicked the "forward" button on my email program - I had clicked "reply-all". Upon receiving the email, Tiger ran over to my desk and asked, "Did you really mean to send that to Judy?"

Of course, I did not. I quickly picked up the phone and called her, in an attempt to apologize as best as I could. She answered the phone with a cheery "Hello?", and I hesitated before responding meekly with "Judy, this is Tony". She quickly replied with "I guess you want to talk to the b**ch in charge?"

I was able to smooth over the situation, but realizing I had shot any chance of a near-future promotion in the proverbial foot, I left the company within a few months.
    ~ Tony Darnell
        Author, *Twenty Forty-Four: The League of Patriots*

IN A CRISIS ... CHOCOLATE

Chocolate doesn't ask
silly questions;
chocolate understands.
~ Unknown

In A Crisis

When I'm in a real shitstorm, I eat chocolate. Does it solve my problems? No. Will it make me feel better? Yes. I have stashes of Rolos and M&M's scattered about my house. I only eat the regular M&M's. I don't judge if you like the pretzel flavor or even the pumpkin spice that they release for the holidays, but I read there's pineapple and Mexican jalapeno in the works and I'm not sure those flavors go with chocolate coated candies. Anyway, whatever your desires are in confections, buy it so when things go down, you're ready.

My good friend, Lise (not a typo, her people are highbrow, it's pronounced Liza) cooks when she's stressed. She says it's impossible for your mind to do two things at once. Lise runs the highly successful blog *MomLovesBaking.com*. I asked her for the EASIEST chocolate recipe, for those of us that are culinary-challenged.

Four-Ingredient M&M Brownies
Serves Nine

Ingredients:

- 1 1/4 cups (371g) Nutella - or one 13-ounce jar
- 2 large eggs room temperature
- 1/2 cup (62g) all-purpose flour
- 1/2 cup (100g) M&M's chocolate candies (Perhaps a cup if there has been a death)

Instructions:

1. Preheat oven to 350°F. Grease an 8"x8" non-stick baking pan. Set aside.
2. Mix the first three ingredients in a large bowl with a wooden spoon until smooth. About 50-60 strokes. Do not over mix. Pour batter into prepared pan and smooth top with a spatula.
3. Sprinkle M&M's candies over batter, distributing evenly. Bake for 20-25 minutes or until a toothpick inserted in center comes out clean. Do not over-bake. Let brownies cool and set before cutting and serving. Cut into nine squares.

I suggest you make a double, or even a triple-batch as I could eat nine brownies for breakfast. For instant gratification, eat the caramel and Nutella as you bake.

I'm not suggesting that chocolate cures us of all our worriment, but you cannot operate in crisis mode non-stop - you have to take a break. So, start with streaming your favorite funny movie and indulge in cherished sweetmeats and renew your soul for a few minutes.

~ Amy Lyle

THEY'RE ANIMALS

I don't understand your specific kind of crazy, but I do admire your total commitment to it.
~ Darynda Jones

That's Not a Snack

I was hiking in the Georgia mountains with my friend, Shannon and our dogs - Shannon's German shorthaired pointer, Truffle, and my golden retriever, Cooper, who were playing in the little creeks and exploring the unknown terrain. It was almost a perfect day until Cooper returned from exploring the creek bank, chomping down on a dirty baby diaper, the contents of which were oozing out both sides. Shannon and I threw up and said nothing during the car ride home.

~ A.L.

Relocation Problem

Our middle-class neighborhood was having raccoon issues. No one wanted to poison or murder the creatures, but they were causing property damage, might have been carrying rabies, and were scaring the wives and children. The men got together to discuss a solution and dubbed the mission "Operation Raccoon Upgrade." The plan was to purchase the Havahart traps, secure them, and then secretly release the racoons several blocks away into a much swankier neighborhood that offered bigger yards, a wooded park, and two ponds.

A few months into "Operation Raccoon Upgrade," I went to a cocktail party at the yacht club. Most of the members were residents of the fancy neighborhood where we had been releasing the raccoons. (I was only at the party because my brother married a blue blood and was forced to include me.) While waiting for a scotch and soda, I overheard a guy - Bill, the richest guy in town - talking about having a raccoon issue. He listed the same issues we had concerns with a few months back about the animals causing property damage, carrying rabies, and scaring the wives and children.

Just as I started to join the conversation, Bill shared his brilliant solution. He said his wife did not want him killing the animals, so he bought the Havahart traps and was dropping them off a few blocks down in MY neighborhood. I asked why he chose that neighborhood, as his neighborhood had the lakes and the trees.

"They have better trash," he replied.
~ Captain Dan from Boston

We'll Take All of Them

While my husband and I were at work, our two Labrador retrievers ate thirty school-fundraising chocolate bars. Because dogs can't easily metabolize theobromine (a component in chocolate), the candy can be toxic. So, we rushed the animals to our veterinarian.

We told him the situation and he asked, "I need to know exactly how many bars each animal consumed."

I said, "I DON'T KNOW! I WASN'T HOME. I don't think they sat down and divided them up beforehand - 'one for you, one for me.'" Luckily, both dogs were fine after the vet worked his magic.

We were just getting over the enormous animal-hospital bill when our kid reminded us we still had to buy all those damn chocolate bars.
    ~ Heather Hobson Terry

Every time the dog farts, he barks, jumps up, and looks at his butt, as if someone has attacked his hiney.
    ~ E.E.

Christmas Sparkle
On Christmas Day, my long-haired cat sauntered by a lit candle and his tail caught on fire. He freaked out and started running around the room. Everybody was chasing after him, clapping their hands up and down his tail to put out the fire.

He wasn't hurt, but he developed severe PTSD. Whenever someone claps, he runs for his life and hides.
    ~ Kathy Riggs Duffy

My Maltese jumped up on the baby's changing table and ate an entire jar of Vaseline. It was quite messy for about a week following that incident.
    ~ Dana Gunn McIntyre

Good Dog

During a day trip to my dad's house, I bent down to hug my dog, Coco Barbara, and she jumped up at the same time and gave me a bloody nose. She also gulped down the fresh venison off the kitchen counter and she ate grandpa's brand-new welcome mat.

~ Jessica Van Derven
Writer, WisconsinTrophyWife.com

Making Matters Worse

I love my Roomba! It has an auto feature that starts it up and it cleans my hardwoods while I'm at work - a super-cool feature on any day ... except the day my dog decides to throw up. It rolled over the vomit and spread it all over my house.

~ Heather Terry

You Must Have Me Confused With Someone Else

After vacation, my family was excited to pick up our golden/Lab, Buddy, from the pet-boarding facility. We thought he was depressed because he didn't seem very excited to see us or the kids. When we arrived home, he wasn't interested in his bed and just pushed his dog food around his bowl. He seemed depressed. We called the vet, who advised we just watch him for a few days.

Buddy finally seemed to be getting back to his old self when the owner of the pet-boarding facility called. "We apologize. We sent you home with the wrong Buddy."

They discovered the issue when the other Buddy's owner arrived and complained about the grooming, saying her dog (a Labrador) was "way too fluffy!" Only upon trying to fix the dog's hairdo did the groomer realize the mix-up.

~ Dana Levent

We're Going to Need an Alpaca

Two days before the photoshoot for this book cover, I saw the sweetest video on social media featuring therapy llamas. The animals were dressed in cute Hawaiian or holiday attire (bunny ears, Santa hats, or even as pilgrims) and would visit children's hospitals and senior-citizen centers. The children and seniors would light up as the llama tried to snuggle them, not unlike a therapy dog, but taller.

I was toggling back and forth, communicating with Andrea, the photographer, on the plan for the photoshoot, when a friend, Amy Spivia, brought to my attention that she knew a woman that raised llamas in the area. AND THEN IT HIT ME: I should have a llama in the studio. I asked her if she could find out if any llamas were available Friday morning, and within minutes, she replied "Yes".

The traits that llamas (and alpacas) are known for lined up beautifully with characteristics of the contributors to this book: naturally curious, friendly and a love for adventure. They also are known to be quite stubborn and if pushed, hostile - which I admire in a person, if it pertains to holding firm to one's beliefs. Another trait is "easily domesticated," but I would not say that is the case for most of my contributors - we're a wilder group. But overall, a llama would be the perfect mascot for the book. That's when the llama farmer called me and told me she was excited about me and my posse visiting her farm.

"What? No, you have to bring the llama to the studio. It wouldn't be funny - me on a farm with a llama - that's its environment."

"NO CAN DO," she said.

Dang it! Now I had everyone's hopes up about a llama. A lack of llamas would change the vibe. I had real llama drama, so Thursday morning I started working the phones. I called vet offices and asked, "Do you have any llama clients? Will you ask them if their llama can be at a studio tomorrow?" A few people said they would call me back. One woman said "yes", but then "no" to the travel. Her llamas were not halter-trained and would be wild and unruly in a studio setting.

Finally, on Thursday at 8:00 pm, at the suggestion of a Facebook friend, I called Carol at Animal Casting Atlanta. I was desperate and would extend my animal reach to include not only a llama, but an ostrich, emu, or worst-case - baby goats. Carol said she had a film shoot south of the city in the afternoon for a movie and announced she did not have any llamas, BUT she could have Aspen the Alpaca at the studio by 10:00 a.m. An alpaca is supposed to be the fluffier, friendlier version of a llama, so we negotiated the fee. (Apparently, animals demand working girls' rates - they charge by the minute. I could only afford Aspen the Alpaca for fifteen minutes.)

Sophie, the alpaca wrangler, showed up to the set on time with Aspen looking beautifully washed with a very puffy hairdo, wearing nothing but a halter. She was a perfect lady, and everyone had a great time. Andrea was able to take some fantastic shots and we were able to create the new cover.

And THAT is why an alpaca is on the cover of the book.
   ~ Amy Lyle

Editor's note: Aspen's name was changed to Santiago for the book's social media campaign.

Check him out at http://facebook.com/amylyle.me

LEGALLY, THEY ARE MY FAMILY

In my family,
crazy is normal.
~ Anonymous

They Start Early

I never imagined that having a boy would require so many discussions about penises. My days are spent like this:

- The grocery store is not an appropriate place to play with your penis.
- Please do not pull your penis out when people are visiting us.
- I know you like your penis, but you need to keep it in your pants while we are at the park.
- Please do not put toys on your penis. Yes, even the big LEGOS. Yes, even blocks.
- Please do not put your penis on the cat.
- I'm videoing you for Grandma. Put your penis away.
  ~ Amy Pierce

Wet Interruptions

I was finishing up a proposal in my office when my wife ran past me, screaming, "Water's shooting out of the dryer!"

"That's impossible," I said, shaking my head in disbelief. "There's no water attached to the dryer." Beach towels in hand, she ran back to the laundry room.

"The house is flooding! Help me!" she yelled.

Irritated, I headed to the laundry room where I saw water pouring out the front of the dryer. I yanked all the soaking-wet clothes out onto the floor and stuck my head into the dryer to see a garden hose spewing. I looked out the window to see the kids playing in the yard, jumping over the hose.

The kids had shoved the hose into the exhaust vent and turned on the water full blast.
~ Martin T.

I Have An Announcement

When my daughter was potty training, she loved to visit EVERY. SINGLE. BATHROOM in EVERY. SINGLE. PLACE we went. She rarely actually went to the potty. I think she enjoyed having my full attention as she sat on the potty and if she even peed one drop, I would praise her.

One morning, we were eating breakfast out at a restaurant. She had finished her milk, drank half of my juice and was working on a glass of water when she said she had to go. She peed and peed. I kept telling her how proud I was.

As we were coming back out of the bathroom, my little 3 year old raised her hands over her head victoriously and shouted (for the entire restaurant to hear) "I WENT PEE-PEE ON THE POTTY FOR A LOOOOONG TIME!"

Everyone around us burst into laughter and clapping. I was mortified, but she was proud as a peacock.
~ J.S. Wood
Author, the "Elena Ransom" young adult fantasy series
JSWood.org

It's Not What It Used to Be

One day, I picked up a fake belly-button ring at Claire's to shock my son. By the time he came home from school, though, I had forgotten about the belly-button ring until I leaned over to pick up a wooden spoon that I had dropped, and my fat roll squished so tightly that the ring shot away from my body like a popping cork, hitting the refrigerator across the room.

My son said, "What was that?" as he picked up the metal clip.

"My belly button ring!" I explained, grabbing it and putting it back on my navel.

He had a look of confusion, disgust and fear as he slowly left the room.

~ Missy Bolt

I Am Much Older Than I Look

My brother and I were cycling when he hit a patch of uneven pavement and crashed. He was holding his head and his knee was bleeding profusely, so I called 911. They asked his age and injuries, I told them he was nineteen and he may have hit his head. At that point my brother said, "I didn't hit my head, I'm fine." I told 911, "He says he's fine." They asked if he was still bleeding and when I said "Yes", they insisted on coming.

The ambulance arrived and the EMT team jumped out the

173

back with the stretcher asking, "Where is he?" I pointed to my brother, who was resting on a bench. The EMT's looked at each other, "Where's the old guy?" I said, "There isn't an old guy, it's my brother." The EMT's started moving their stretcher back to the ambulance, before they left one commented, "We thought you said he was ninety."

~ Ellen M.

Wrong Number
My phone pinged with a text message from my seventy-year-old stepmom, Nancy, an uptight Southern woman who would frown upon using the word "pregnant" in mixed company. With all her rules and lectures about being prim and proper, I was taken aback to see that her text read, "It's always good in our new bed." She was sexting my father!

I forwarded the text to him and his reply was, "Naughty Nancy" … and a string of smiling emojis.

~ C.H.

They Do Everything Together
My son was barely three and newly potty-trained, and he had to go. He ran to the bathroom and his dog Trigger (lemon beagle) followed him. I casually walked by to check on him and saw the dog drinking from the toilet bowl - while my son was peeing. I screamed.

"He drinks from the fountain," my son stated flatly.

"That's gross," I replied. "The dog shouldn't drink your pee. Flush the toilet so the dog has clean water." I walked away and heard the toilet flush, but when they didn't come out of the bathroom, I checked back. The dog was sitting there patiently, staring at my son whose head was completely in the toilet.

"Get out of there!" I screeched. "What are you doing?"

"I flushed," my son replied. "We're taking turns."
    ~ Nicole S.

Falsely Quirky

My sister-in-law's parakeet was at our house because my mother-in-law (who lived with us) was bird-sitting while they were on a trip. My sister-in-law kept Facetiming the bird. She didn't even like the bird, but she kept telling people how incredibly quirky she was because she called to talk to the bird.

No one really likes her or the bird.
    ~ N.G.

Oy Vey

It was late December and my family had just relocated to Atlanta from Florida. We had been up since 5:00 a.m. unpacking all the moving boxes. Both my husband and I were getting cranky because the children were refusing to go to bed until we located their special blankets, which

I must have mislabeled because there were no more boxes that read "Girls' bedrooms."

We finally put the kids in bed, and my husband headed to the shower. I poured a cup of bubble bath in the tub, put my hair in a clear shower cap, and stepped into the tub. The second I exhaled, the doorbell rang. We ignored it, but it kept ringing. We both grabbed our robes and headed downstairs, but our kids beat us to the door.

Standing in front of us were ten Christmas-caroling children. I almost closed the door at the halfway mark of "Hark the Herald Angels Sing" (because I still had my shower cap and robe on), but then the carolers' parents, who were at the bottom of our driveway, started walking up the hill. Finally, the song was over, and the parents wished us a merry Christmas. The carolers then started humming "We Wish You a Merry Christmas," but my husband and I thanked everyone and apologized that we had to go because, as they could see, we were in the middle of our showers.

Before we closed the door, a woman asked if we wanted to carol with the group tomorrow. "Not tomorrow," I said. "We're still getting settled."

"Are you going to see Santa at the clubhouse?" she inquired. I shook my head no.

After a pause, another woman asked, "Where will you be attending church?"

My husband and I were quiet. We stared at the humming carolers and their parents and they stared back and then finally my husband said, "We're Jews. We attended Temple Beth Shalom."

The carolers stopped humming and left. When our doorbell rang a few days later, it was a mom of one of the carolers, delivering her attempt at a Jewish dish, noodle kugel.

It's actually a Passover dish, but we appreciated the welcoming gesture.
~ L.B.

There's Something in the Water

My family used to spend a few weeks every summer at Watch Hill on picturesque Fire Island, NY, which is only accessible by boat. It has a beautiful beach that's practically empty and exclusive before the ferry dumps the tourists off.

When I was a young teen, I went to the beach early one morning with my sister and a friend, and the ocean was full of amazing foam. It was really something to see. Naturally, we jumped in and covered ourselves with the foam. We made hats out of it. We threw it at each other. We were each completing our ZZ Top-style beards, using the foam, when three grown men approached us.

Two were waving their arms wildly and yelling, "Get out of the water! Dear God, that's dangerous! No swimming, no swimming!" The third guy was holding a sign. In a panic, we all rushed out of the water, ZZ Top beards and all, thinking for sure there was a Jaws-sized great white in the water.

"Is it a shark?" I asked. The three men looked at each other and shook their heads. At that point the third guy turned his sign around to post into the ground.

It read, "Danger! Sewage Water. No Fishing. No Drinking. No Swimming."
~ E.M.

1978 Halloween Dream

I grew up in the tiny town of Reno, Ohio, a town so small we didn't have street numbers. My address was simply "Star Route." To the right of my house was a church built in the 1800's that Mildred and George Cady, who had three girls, had converted into a home. Other than the Cady's, we had no other neighbors closer than a mile. Directly across the road, and for miles behind my house, was a cattle farm. More than once I stepped off the school bus to see a full-grown cow munching on grass in my front yard, having escaped its fence. To the left were acres of feed corn used to feed the livestock.

My sister and I only participated in Halloween a few times growing up. My mom told me it was because the area was so rural all the candy would be gone by the time we drove from house to house. But my father raised the real objections – he did not want to waste gas driving us around and he thought ringing doorbells to ask for candy were the activities of beggars. Together, my parents bribed my sister and me into not participating for years by getting us each a candy bar from the store and letting us pick out one item from the three-inch-thick JCPenney catalog that came in the mail once a quarter.

The candy and catalog item satisfied us until we were six and seven, but when all our friends bragged about their amazing outfits and how they got so much candy they had to organize it, we rebelled. It was the night before Halloween 1978.

At first, we tried our "everyone else gets to go" strategy, but my parents had built up resistance to that argument over the years. I thought we were beat until my sister rallied on grounds that not participating in Halloween was "un-American." My mother rolled her eyes, but it must have struck a chord with our previously military father, who told us to get into the Buick.

We went into town, and the good news for my dad was all the costumes were on sale. The bad news for my sister and me was the selection was very limited. We both ran to the only girl costumes available, Daisy Duke from the Dukes of Hazzard and one Sabrina Duncan from Charlie's Angels. (Sabrina was the least sexy of the Angels trio.) As my sister and I started to argue over who would get Daisy or Sabrina, my mother told us that both costumes were too provocative for little girls to wear.

The second we started to protest, my father grabbed two boxed costume sets and headed to the checkout station. In the car, I was handed an Incredible Hulk outfit. I was about to complain until my sister got her outfit, Jimmy Carter.

We asked to trick or treat in town, as there were rows of homes close together. My mother said "No" on the grounds we did not have our pillowcases to collect our candy, and my father said it wouldn't be fair because "we don't pay city taxes." My sister and I were only in first and second grade and didn't have the data needed to question the Halloween city-taxes argument.

My mom ran into the house to grab two pillowcases and we were off! The first house we went to was everything we had ever dreamed of: a nice lady gave us full-size Three Musketeers bars and a handful of Dubble Bubble. The second house had a long, steep driveway. We both were so hot in our plastic, garbage-bag costumes with only a tiny airhole to breathe through in the masks. When we lifted the masks to inhale, our elastics snapped, so we had to hold our masks on with one hand while waving our

Holly Hobbie pillowcases in front of the candy distributors. By the fifth house, our garbage-bag costumes had been caught in the car door and were ripped. We totally lost our steam by the tenth stop, when a group of older girls, decked out as Farrah Fawcett's "Jill Munroe" from Charlie's Angels, made fun of our pillowcases and broken Hulk and Jimmy Carter ensembles.

We dumped our candy on the living room floor, put on the Grease record and organized our stash into piles: chocolate with filling, chocolate with nuts, Nerds and Necco wafers, Pixy Stix, Pop Rocks, and fruits (raisins and apples).

My mom came in and asked us to give her all the candy. She would dole it out to us in our lunches because she didn't want our teeth to "rot out of our heads." We complained of hunger, which landed us a spot at the kitchen table eating Crock-Pot-soaked Vienna sausages.

We never asked to go trick or treating again.
    ~ Amy Lyle

Now I Remember

My brother is a dentist, but my whole family treats him like a general practitioner and calls him for everything from sore throats to urinary tract infections. One morning, I was hungover from the night before, but sicker than I had ever been. I called my brother to tell him I was throwing up a lot of blood. He told me to go to the emergency room immediately.

It wasn't until my husband offered me a bottle of water in the hospital that I realized I had made an expensive mistake. I was NOT throwing up blood. The night before at a game party, the signature drink was a "bloody roadrunner," made of Gatorade, Southern Comfort and Hawaiian Punch.

~ Won't let me use her name because her mother
   would be disappointed

He's Worth the Wait
My mother-in-law is in love with a convicted felon that she had met through the Meet-an-Inmate.com. Her pal's name is Erwin. She said, "He's in the big house for *messy financial matters*," but we researched the public records and discovered he's in for robbing a dozen banks. She talks about their future life together "once the truth is revealed," but he's not eligible for release until 2069. She'll be 118 when he gets out. At first, I tried to discourage the relationship. I feared a prisoner may take advantage of a lonely woman, but she seems happy and the only thing Erwin has ever asked her to buy him are used books and new socks.

~ Bes D.

One Day Only
My husband had been traveling for work for the last week, and I had a slight case of the blues, feeling isolated

at home with a brand-new baby. Scanning the paper, I saw an ad for professional baby portraits being offered for "One-day only" at the Holiday Inn, which was less than a few blocks from where I lived. I called, set the appointment, and reported to room 31.

The second the photographer opened the door, I regretted booking the session. "Stan" was at least seventy, and he had terrible brown teeth and a thin, greasy comb-over. It looked like he had been living in the hotel room; there was a rice cooker on the counter and dirty clothes piled up against the wall.

He asked me to pick out some props. On one of the beds he offered baby rattles to full-size baseball bats. I selected a rattle and he took a few shots. When I went to get my son, he asked me if I wanted any nude pictures.

I replied, "No thank you," and handed him thirty dollars in cash. He grabbed a large scrapbook from the counter and kept flipping the pages, showing me all the other naked baby pictures he had taken.

It was when he offered to take them for free that I believed my son and I would be murdered. I was already thinking about my son's tiny coffin and how my husband would have to answer the question, "Why would she do that?" for the rest of his life. I told Stan that my mother was waiting in the car for me and I needed to check on her. When he told me he needed my address to mail the pictures, I ran out.

I didn't tell my husband the story until my kid was graduating from high school.

~ Julie J

Adjustment of Screen Time

Our eight-year-old son, Sam, had been begging for a phone or a tablet since he was five, but we felt he wasn't responsible enough. When my husband won an iPad at work, though, we decided to gift his older iPad to Sam with the caveat that he could only play games and watch shows we approved. When Sam requested animated movies such as *How to Train Your Dragon* and the *Despicable Me* series, we were relieved that he was still very much into "kid" movies with good messages.

Almost a year went by and we had few issues with Sam getting into any bad content. In fact, we loved that he was extending from cartoons to the NASA Space Program and the lives of reptiles. He also showed great interest in all sorts of leaders in the world, such as Dr. Martin Luther King, J. Edgar Hoover, and Winston Churchill, as he would incorporate their most common sayings into his daily life. (For example, he would tell his nine-month-old sister, Eliza, to, "Never, never, never give up.")

We started to think, though, that his interest in the famed FBI director, J. Edgar Hoover, had sparked an interest in crime. We were at a friend's house, visiting their kitten, when Sam asked, matter-of-factly, as he gently pet the tabby, "If I pulled this cat's tail out, would it die, or could it be sewn back on?" I told him it would really hurt the kitty and it was time to go.

Over the next few days, he would ask the most morbid questions about people getting electrocuted and how big would a freezer need to be to put a body in it. We thought he might have a serious problem until we checked his viewing history. Sam had moved away from animal shows and research and was binge-watching *NCIS*, *Criminal Minds* and *Grey's Anatomy*.

We now limit his iPad time to an hour a day.
~ R.D.

Pony Rides
When our kids were little we were so broke I would not spare the quarter to let them ride the kiddie horse outside the Piggly Wiggly. Instead, I would perch two of them in the saddle and tell them to shake the reins, move their legs in the stirrups, and say, "Giddy-up!" I would grab the tail of the horse and shake it as hard as I could to make them think the machine was on.

Coming out of the grocery store, my kids saw a boy on the same horse that was now going up and down and making clip-clop and neighing sounds. My kids started screaming, "Mommy, look at the horse! What is it doing?"

I told them it was broken and corralled them to the car.
　~ J. Callahan

She's Very Upset
Every summer, my parents would pack up my sister, two brothers and me and head to Cape San Blas for a week. Their lifelong friends, Charlie and Barbara, plus their four kids would join us in a giant house that sat right on the beach. Their son, Ben, was a year older than me and for over twenty years I dreamed we would get married and continue the summer trips with our own family.

My favorite part of the trip, even more than hanging out with Ben, was listening to Mr. Charlie's stories at dinner. He had been a writer and filmmaker and shared his onset experiences about how wonderful or dreadful certain stars were to work with, disagreements with producers, and all the crazy happenings during his travels. He would always start his tales with, "Remember, Barbara?"

Barbara was also a writer and had been on too many movie sets to count. They would sometimes start giggling so hard, remembering an event, that it would take them a few minutes to compose themselves. The love they shared had to be admired.

Years later, we were all gathered back together for a great

loss. Charlie, close to eighty, fought stomach cancer for two years before he finally succumbed. My siblings and I flew in from all over the country to attend the service. After the funeral, Barbara's daughter, Jen, held a lovely lunch for family and friends at her home in Atlanta.

As I was catching up with my childhood crush, Ben, we both noticed his mother acting strange. She was welcoming guests into the house and then excusing herself to "get some lunch." Several times we saw her eating plates of baked ham, beans, rolls and desserts.

I mentioned to Ben, "I believe that's her third plate. Do you think she's alright?"

Ben took a deep breath and flatly said, "Mom's totally stoned."

Sweet Barbara was so upset about the loss of her husband she had started taking his medicinal marijuana. She had taken a large dose in anticipation of the wake and was high out of her mind.
    ~ S.K.

Is That Contagious?
Riding in the car with several twelve-year-olds, returning from a long day of lacrosse, I finally dropped off the last girl. My daughter commented on how fantastic, Jen, the newest player on the team, had played.

"She has A LOT of energy," she continued. "Even after four games in a row, she would jog in place on the sidelines. Mom, she literally cannot stop moving around. I think she has an STD."

"You mean ADD?" I asked.

"I'm not sure, Mom," my daughter said. "I just know she can't stop, and she may have a disease."

~ S.K.

You May Need a Trim

One of my husband's dreams finally came true when we were able to purchase a boat. On the maiden voyage, we gathered all our family members and filled every seat on the pontoon. We towed kids on tubes around the coves and everyone was enjoying the day. In between switching kids out on the tube, a few people jumped in the water to get cooled off.

My mother-in-law, Judy, made a dramatic splash as she cannon-balled into the lake. Everyone swam around for twenty minutes and climbed back into the boat. Judy was the last one to get back in, as she was having trouble getting up the ladder. She would go up a few steps and then fall back into the water. Everyone on the boat was laughing because she was laughing. The kids starting videoing her and giving her words of encouragement. Finally, with a huge grunt, she pulled herself up and was back on the deck.

I was getting a towel from the back of the boat when everything went silent. I asked, "What's wrong?" as I turned and saw my mother-in-law, still smiling, not knowing that her bathing suit did not provide enough coverage and the natural state of her pubic hair was revealed for all to see. I threw a towel at her and we headed back to the dock.

~ S.A.

Don't Test Me

While pulling my teenage daughter's clothes out of the dryer, I discovered a plastic baggie of what looked like weed. When she returned home from school, I showed her the bag.

"If you don't want me to smoke weed, I won't," she said.

"You're telling me that before today you didn't know you weren't supposed to smoke weed?" my husband asked. She shrugged her shoulders and looked at her feet. "We're going to start drug-testing you. If you test positive, you'll lose the use of the car." She nodded.

"I don't want to waste a drug test. We know if you take one now, it will come back as positive," he said as he looked at the directions on the drug screening box. "Tell me when you could pass a drug screening."

She replied, "What do you mean, when will I be able to pass a drug test?"

"It takes a while for the drugs to leave your system, so when should we test you?" he asked.

"How many days does it take for it to get out of your system?" asked our daughter.

"About thirty days," my husband answered. "So when can we test you?"

She looked him and said, "Thirty days."
~ P.F.

As Sweet as Peaches

My mother, a debutante from the East Coast, had fallen in love with my cattle-farmer father she had met in a grocery store in Mississippi. They got married and had five of us kids; I have three brothers and one sister. To help my mother, my father hired a nanny, Miss Mae, to care for us a few days a week so that my mother could go into town to have lunch and play bridge with a few friends.

Our house sat on thousands of acres, but my parents built it within a stone's throw of a four-lane highway and railroad tracks. Although there was a lot of traffic, many trains and dangerous farm equipment around, my siblings and I were allowed to roam free on the farm, so Mae spent her days protecting us from sure death and telling us "NO!" at least a thousand times a day.

Like clockwork, my mother would return at four-thirty in the afternoon. As she hung up her coat, she would ask Mae how we behaved. Miss Mae would tell my mom the same lie every time: "Your children are the sweetest I have ever known. They're angels." Mae worked for us for a couple of years, until her mother got sick and she had to leave to care for her in another state.

My father hired another nanny, Miss Jenny, to patrol us on Mom's bridge days. Returning from town, my mother hung up her jacket as usual and asked the new nanny how we behaved. Miss Jenny said, as she grabbed her own jacket off the rack, that we were "The worst children in the world" and that she had never seen such rotten kids. My mom nodded in agreement and asked if she was coming back next week.

"Yes," she said, begrudgingly, "I'll be back." and walked out the door. Miss Jenny stayed with us for almost a decade.
~ Shaun Swedenberg

Just Breathe

My people are Irish. We drink, we're loud and we love a great debate with other family members. When my brother married, he brought into the family a sweet, demure woman, Maja, that he had met in the library while at college. They had four kids under the age of ten, and I had never heard her raise her voice to any of them. If my brother (her husband) was getting too rowdy, she would simply say, "Patrick, please settle down."

The sternest comment I heard her dole out to their kids was to their middle child, Laney, who was going through an argumentative stage and would refuse to eat anything offered at the table. For Thanksgiving, Maja had prepared a beautiful meal and we were gathering to say prayers and eat when Laney started complaining.

"That is a dead bird. That's disgusting! What's that gross brown stuff? It looks like poo." We all held our tongues, waiting to see what Maja would do.

She bent down, got eye to eye with Laney, and said so quietly that we had to strain to hear her, "Laney love, if you do not like what is offered, you may go to your room after we say the prayer." She then held Laney's hand and deferred to her husband, who said a blessing, and we sat down. Laney stomped to her room.

As the holiday crowd dispersed and Maja was putting the kids to bed, it was just my brother and I finishing up the last of the dishes. I asked him, "I've never seen such a calm human being. How can she handle you, the kids and our crazy family without even raising an eyebrow?"

My brother looked around the room, as if he might find some eavesdroppers. He put his hands to his lips and motioned me to the laundry room, which was just past the kitchen. He pulled out a stepladder, moved a stack of fabric-softener boxes, and handed me a box from the back of the stack. It smelled like lavender.

"You are so full of it," I said. "Don't give me that organic, essential-oil crap. I don't care how much lavender you smell, it's not going to …" I stopped when I opened the box. The decade-long mystery of how my sister-in-law could remain so calm had been solved.

In the lavender, organic fabric-softener box was a giant bag of weed.
　　~ S.N.

Your Dad and I Are Getting Busy

I drove 2,000 miles from Montana to Mississippi to visit my parents, and when I finally arrived and knocked on the door several times, no one answered. I knew they were home, as I saw my dad's old truck and my mom's Jeep in the driveway. Just when I turned to get back into my car, the door cracked open.

My seventy-seven-year-old mother stood there in a bright-yellow robe. "You're early," she said, refusing to open the door for me to enter.

"Mom, I've driven thirty hours in the last two days," I said. "Open the door."

My mother took a deep breath and stated flatly, "Your dad has taken his Viagra. They cost six dollars apiece and we don't want to waste it. Come back in twenty minutes."
~ Shaun Swedenberg

Strange Conditions
We were in the middle of a midweek family dinner when my youngest son, Matthew, who was ten, made an announcement. "I have lost my puberty," he said. I bit my tongue and waited. "The nurse told me a secret," he continued.

Alarms struck. Who was this secret nurse and why was she talking to him about puberty? After more questioning, I discovered that the "nurse" was his female pediatrician who completed his wellness checkup over five months ago. The doctor, during a normal exam, pressed on his abdominal area and made a comment about puberty.

Michael thought he was dying from something growing in his stomach, a disease called "puberty." For months he had been checking it day and night, and he now knew that he was healed. It was gone. He had finally lost his puberty. He then asked his father to pass the green beans and we all enjoyed our dinner.
~ Jimmy B.

We're Trying to Help You

Our son gets hazed by his older sisters constantly because he does not shave as frequently as they would like him to. On the way to school, they were razzing him about his scruffy, ratty "neck beard." He would always have the same muffled reply, "Shut it."

Finally, our oldest daughter tried to reason with him. "Look, you are at best a seven when you are completely showered, clean-shaven and have on a decent outfit. With the neck beard, you drop to a five. No chicks will like you."

He looked to his other sister for support, but unfortunately, she was nodding in agreement with their sister. "I think a five is stretch, you're maybe a four" she told him.

~ Maddy L.

The Latest News

My wife and I make an effort to expose our children to our country's past. We balance vacations at the beach and theme parks with learning the history of the area. When our oldest, Amelie, who was ten, started taking a real interest in how the events impacted people, we were delighted. The combination of our trips and her fourth-grade history lessons started to be hot topics at the dinner table.

"What happened to the Roanoke colonists?" she would ask, as well as, "Why did the white people take all the Indians' land?" I was thrilled when she started researching historical events online and presenting her findings daily at dinner. We started to have aspirations that her passion for others' suffering might lead her to become an activist or attorney.

One week, when she joined us for dinner, her face evoked that she had discovered yet another disappointing event in history. She calmly folded her napkin on her lap, took a deep breath, and began. "In 1912, the most luxurious passenger ship in the world, the Titanic, struck an iceberg and sunk in Newfoundland."

"Yes," her mother and I said in unison, waiting for her diatribe about how fifteen hundred people lost their lives due to their lack of social status.

Amelie continued, "Why in the world would Rose push Jack off that door when there was plenty of room for both of them?" I didn't know what she was referring to until my wife filled me in on the dramatic Leo DiCaprio and Kate Winslet freezing-water scene in the two-billion-dollar blockbuster *Titanic* movie.

~ Dan Watts

I Scream, You Scream, We All Scream for Ice Cream

After the holidays, my mother and I discovered we had both gained about ten pounds, so we planned to lose the weight together, making a commitment to try the meal-replacing SlimFast shakes for seven days. The plan requires you to drink two shakes a day in place of meals. The seven days were excruciating for me. I like to chew - not drink - food. However, I lost five pounds and was excited to reveal my results to my mom at dinner.

"These don't work! I've gained six pounds this week!" she screamed at me.

"Gained? You only get two a day. How many have you been drinking?"

My mother reared up indignantly at my accusation that she was not following the directions. "Two," she said firmly. As I was thinking about how to reply, she added, "And I was only using two scoops of ice cream in them."
    ~ Beth A.

Oh Snap!

My husband, Randal, and I used to have a boat, which we would take out on the lake almost every day in the summer. When we first got the boat, we parked it in our driveway and covered it with a tarp secured with bungee cords. Randal asked me not to touch the bungee cords because I was not "mechanically inclined."

Bungee cords are not mechanical, so when the tarp was laid out, I grabbed the first cord I saw and started pulling. I was stretching it - really hard - to reach the trailer. Before I knew it, I was on the ground, my glasses were broken, and I saw blood. I felt like I had been shot. I touched my face and my eyebrow was bleeding. Thank goodness my glasses had protected my eyes.

To this day, almost a decade later, if there is a bungie cord in sight Randal will look at me and say, "Don't touch that."
~ Brooke and Randal Fowler
Married AF podcast

That's Not What I Meant

Pulling up to my patient visit, I popped the trunk to retrieve some files. As I closed the trunk, I saw that my twelve-year-old had drawn a very large penis into the winter sludge coating my vehicle. When I went home, I asked her to please stop drawing giant penises on my car and she agreed.

The next afternoon, as I headed out, I saw more drawings on my car. After inspecting them, I shook my head, appreciating that my daughter did not draw a giant penis.

She had drawn at least twenty tiny penises.
~ Amanda Redhead

Bye-Bye Birdies

As my family and I were excusing ourselves from a lovely wedding reception, the mother of the bride walked us out. I apologized for having to leave, but we had another engagement to get to; the men in the family had gone quail hunting a few weeks back and they were having a quail cook-off of sorts.

The mother of the bride said, "Oh, quail are such lovely birds. As children, in the 1950's, we raised quail and gave them away as Christmas gifts."

"As pets, in cages?" I asked.

"No," she said flatly. "Frozen, in butcher paper. They're delicious with bacon."
~ Barbara C.

I Can See Your Noodle

For summer vacation, we were taking the kids to Gatlinburg, Tennessee to escape the Atlanta heat, and I was excited to return to a place my family had taken us as kids. I loved the small, sleepy town that offered winding hiking trails and front-porch rocking chairs on the mountain chalet rentals. As we entered Gatlinburg, I realized it had changed dramatically. There were chain restaurants and the streets were lit with neon signs advertising rental properties, Dollywood tickets, and T-shirt shops.

We were meeting my parents and my in-laws, or as my husband and I affectionately called them, The Baptists. They were very strict, modest, teetotalers from the Deep South that did not like any shenanigans. The first night went great; we enjoyed an amazing dinner, and all got settled into our rooms. Saturday morning, we hiked and then strolled along the strip, collecting brochures, and our group found ourselves a family divided between visiting *Ripley's Believe It or Not* and going on the ski lift.

As my husband was petitioning that we do both, one that day and one the next, a bee flew up his shorts and was stinging his genitals. He started dancing around, pulling at his crotch area and screaming, "My balls!" and "Bee! Bee!" His father, a practical man, started whacking his shorts with a stack of brochures and, in a panic, his mother pulled down his sports shorts. A dead bee fell to the sidewalk.

It seemed like a thousand people had stopped and stared in wonderment. My husband had chosen nylon shorts with built-in underwear so that he "Wouldn't bunch" on the hike. He now stood half-naked on the city streets of Gatlinburg.

My mother-in-law, whom I had never heard utter a curse word, broke the silence. "Sweet Jesus, pull up your shorts. We can see your noodle." It was a very quiet ride with the family back up the long, mountain road.
    ~ Charlotte M.

Who's the Goat?

My fellow interns and I were finishing up our last days with an online publisher. It had been a rough summer. Our manager, the editor, who had just started with the group a few weeks before we did, was totally incompetent. The magazine was online and offline constantly due to server issues, the biggest advertiser had pulled out because their website was spelled wrong in the ads, and no one was bringing in new business. It felt as if the future of the magazine had been given to us, the unpaid grunts.

It was at this time that he pulled us into the "conference room" (it was the break room unless the door was closed; then it was the conference room). We thought he might be extending our internships into part-time positions or, at a minimum, offer us thank-you coffee gift cards to show his appreciation for taking on much more than the job description implied.

Instead, in whispered tones, he admitted that he had made a few errors as the manager and the owner of the company was coming in to address the issues. He explained that contracts had been blundered, policies had not been followed and he could be fired. We asked if there was anything we could do to help him.

He cheered up and said, "Yes." He said that he was the one with the family and really needed a job, so he would like us to resign, effective immediately, and that he would be using us as "escaped goats." When we told him that the term was "scapegoat," he said, "Yes, YOU are the escaped goats. You're escaping when you resign." We walked off the job and never heard from him again.

~ Todd M.

IT ALL HAPPENED IN THE CAR

I like nonsense,
it wakes up the brain cells.
~ Dr. Seuss

It Wasn't My Father's Chevy

I woke up to something rare in the state of Georgia - below-freezing temperatures, snow and ice. Already running late for school, I jumped into my car and turned the defroster on full blast. With the clock ticking, I could see only a tiny sliver of road through the icy windshield. As I backed out, I would need to drive slowly to let the motor get warm, so by the time I arrived at the main intersection, the ice would have melted enough so I could see out the front. Suddenly, I heard the loudest metal-against-metal CRUNCH. A car was parked almost in front of our driveway and I had backed into it.

I jumped out and saw what looked like a junkyard Chevy - the same model my father had from the seventies. One window was taped up with cardboard, the muffler was dragging, and it had dents all over it. I knew it was wrong, but I was running so late; plus, I reasoned that the car already had so many scratches and dents, what was one more? I backed around it and went toward school. My mind started racing. What if I did damage to their car? Whose car was it? Is it illegal to not leave a note?

I was only a block from school when I heard sirens. By then, my car had completely defrosted, and I could clearly see the police car behind me with its lights on. I pulled over. When the officer approached my window, I was weeping, holding my driver's license and insurance card. The police officer said, "Miss, did you know—" And then I cut him off, crying about how I did know, but I was so late for school and I knew what I did was wrong, but I was scared I would get in trouble … and on and on.

The officer said, "That's enough. I won't give you a ticket this time, but do not coast through stop signs." I stopped sobbing and waited. He continued, "You must always come to a full stop."

~ L.A.B.

Send Them to the Fishes

My husband was researching things to do in Gatlinburg, Tennessee, and got his mind set on going to Ripley's Aquarium. Everyone was excited to check out all the creatures and get a break from the heat. Our debate was whether we should eat before we went, which was how the women voted, or whether we should skip the prep and cleanup and just eat at the venue, which was what the kids and the men wanted to do. My husband said he would pick up the tab, so his mother finally agreed; we were off to see the fishes.

The aquarium offered fast-food fare, so we all got either pizza or a hamburger, except my husband, who decided to "be healthy" and get a pre-made salad. About an hour later, Dale was curled over with severe abdominal pains, saying his appendix must be bursting. An aquarium employee approached us and asked if he should call an ambulance. Meanwhile, another employee said not to call an ambulance because it would take over an hour to arrive and it would be faster to drive him to the hospital ourselves.

An aquarium employee brought us a wheelchair, and Dale's father pushed him to the exit as I ran and pulled the car around. As the employees were trying to help Dale into the car, I was frantically looking up the hospital on my phone. An employee said, "Ma'am, just turn left at Dollywood and you'll run into the hospital."

As we entered the hospital, there were tons of patients filling up the emergency room with everything from broken ankles to one mountain man that said he "stepped on a trap," revealing what was left of his bloodied foot. Finally, after an hour, Dale was called back. The hospital was so busy they warned us that he would have to share a room, but the whole family was just grateful a doctor was finally going see Dale.

The family waited along the halls because the waiting room was overflowing as Dale was lifted into a bed. Even in his pain, Dale noticed that there was a police officer standing next to his "roommate's" bed. Within seconds there was chaos. The doctor came in and pushed on my husband's stomach, asking, "What's the pain level here?"

At the same time, the "roommate" was wailing at the doctor that he "Needed his f****** cigarettes." Dale's mom was peeking through the door, clutching her heart with one hand and covering her mouth with the other, despairing of her son's pain. Meanwhile, the roommate had, in his thrashing about cigarettes, ripped the curtain that had separated them to reveal that he had one hand handcuffed to the bed. He was obviously a felon. The police officer put his hands on the felon's shoulders and screamed, "Shut up, shut up!"

My husband screamed in agony as the doctor pushed on his abdomen, and the room fell silent. "We may have to operate," the physician said to a nurse, who immediately started typing into a handheld device. I could hear Dale's mom saying the Lord's prayer to herself behind me when Dale, being turned on his right side by the physician, let out a stream of flatulence that lasted at least ten seconds. His mother collapsed into her husband's arms as all of us tried not to laugh. The convict, however, screamed, "Dear God, was that a fart?"

Hours later, after Dale had his appendix removed and was happily in a dream state from whatever pain medication they were administering in his drip, a quiet came over the entire family for several minutes. It was interrupted by our kids taking turns imitating their grandmother, repeating, "Dear God, was that a fart?" and then laughing hysterically. We have not been back to Gatlinburg in ten years.

~ Charlotte M.

There's No Stopping Me

I had an important meeting and asked my husband if we could trade my Honda for his Mercedes for the day. Reluctantly, he agreed, as I had a less than perfect driving record. I took the keys and headed to the driveway. As I was backing out, I was also trying to adjust the seat, to pull it closer to the steering wheel. I jerked it forward, too close, and then backwards, but it took off and went all the way to the back of the track. I could no longer reach the pedals, AND with the seat belt locked so tightly, I couldn't move. My feet were not on the pedals, but I was still in reverse. I looked to see my husband staring at me from the window. We locked eyes as I slowly backed into our neighbor's mailbox.

~ C.W.C.

I Can't Hold It Together

I have a little travel anxiety, especially if I'm the driver. When my husband had an upcoming extended business trip, I finally succumbed to my mother's pleas to visit her in Alabama. Without traffic, the trip was a little over three hours.

I loaded my toddler daughter and infant son into their car seats, packed a few snacks and hit the road. I had barely left my neighborhood when both kids started crying. I sang to them, played soothing music and offered treats … to no avail. Finally, after about two hours of nonstop wailing, both children fell asleep.

I started to relax until I realized I had to pee. If I pulled over, I would have to wake up the kids. Even if I locked the car door and ran into a rest-stop bathroom, they could wake up (because the car stopped) and cry for hours. My mind was racing as I took short breaths, trying to decide what to do other than pee my pants.

As I checked the status of the kids in the rearview mirror, I noticed the diaper bag between them. Without even slowing down, I reached behind me and grabbed a diaper that was sticking out the top of the bag. I opened it and shoved it down my pants. I know I peed for at least thirty-five seconds because I started to slowly count "one-Mississippi, two-Mississippi" to calm myself. Baby diapers are remarkably absorbent, and as I removed what felt like a five-pound diaper, I was completely dry.

~ Lily S.

WORST GIFTS EVER

I walk around
like everything is fine,
but deep down,
inside my shoe,
my sock is sliding off.
~ Katherine Bainbridge

Corny Gift

My passive-aggressive ex-in-laws gave me a Butter Boy for Christmas. They thought it was the most innovative kitchen gadget ever invented. They demonstrated how you open the bottom and stick the butter in the boy's butt and then spread it over  corn on the cob. When I reminded them that I was allergic to corn, they waved me off like I was kidding.

~ Misty Sunshine

No Thank You

My great-grandparents always had a big Thanksgiving get-together. After the meal, names were drawn for a gift exchange for when the family got together again at Christmas. My mother would decline to put our names in the bowl, saying that she couldn't commit to us being there since she was a police officer and we lived so far away. Every year, we would show up for Christmas and watch my cousins open their amazing gifts. My great-grandma would try to make things better by running to her room, grabbing something they weren't using - a man's wallet, a half bottle of decade-old cologne, or a crocheted Easter-egg pincushion - and pretend it was my gift.

~ Mia Moore

Our Family Has Diverse Talents

My dad's side of the family is known for their "unusual" gifts. Most were from the dollar store or flea market, but

I think the most memorable were T-shirts from a company my aunt was starting up. She caught fish, painted them, and pressed them onto shirts. It was dead-fish fashion. Another aunt made us Santa Claus ornaments out of dried okra (she has her own Facebook page featuring them). My favorite was the homemade beaded jewelry made by my dad's cousin who was serving time in prison, but my mom confiscated it - she said it was the work of the devil.

~ Contributor asked that I use "Lower Alabama."

Oh Lord

My grandmother liked to gift my entire family wares with Jesus on them, from coffee mugs to holiday sweaters. She would seem so happy, even though she knew our family was not religious whatsoever. She would remind us, "That's our Lord."

~ B. Harralson

No Cheer Here

My worst gift was divorce papers. He even wrapped them to be a smartass.

~ Jessica K.

Tell Me Why

When I was fourteen, I received an iguana for Christmas, even though I had never expressed any interest in herbivorous lizards or any other reptile. I named him Smaug. He lived to be six years old and over four feet long.

~ C K.

No Matchy Match

The in-laws gave me a stack of fifteen brand-new (but not matching) bath towels. My mom made me hold up every towel while she commented, "Oh, that's nice, a blue one with fringe!" and "Look at the yellow one with the birds - just lovely. Aren't they wonderful, Erin?"

~ Erin E.

Thank You, Again

My grandmother gets us one of those static sweepers, a nonstick frying pan, and an emergency lantern EVERY YEAR for Christmas. My mother told us to be polite and act surprised. We donated it all to a charity after the holidays.

~ S.G.

Modern Art

A few years ago, I received two large, framed prints. One was a cat wearing a nun's habit, depicting Mother Teresa. The other was a bulldog, dressed as Rembrandt. They are displayed prominently in my stairwell and have been wonderful conversation pieces because they are so very hideous.

~ B. Harralson

But It's Staring At Me

We had moved in the summer of 1967 to a small town in a different state. We quickly became friends with Jo and Jerry, who had three kids close to the same age as ours.

Around Valentine's day a couple years later, I received a large and heavy box, wrapped in thick white paper, and with a huge bow on the top. The card was signed "To my dear friend Bunny, love Jo."

I was a little taken aback, because we had never exchanged gifts with one another, and I had not planned on giving her anything for Valentine's day.

The family gathered around for the big unveiling, and as I opened the box, a horrific stench filled the room. I looked inside to see a very real and very raw pig's head. When I called my friend to "thank her" for the gift, she said "I saw this in the grocery store and it made me think of you."

~ Bunny D.

WE'RE ALL A MESS, IT'S OK

You're entirely bonkers.
But I'll tell you a secret.
All the best people are.
~ Lewis Carroll

The Story Behind the Stories

I shared with a very special Facebook group the purpose of this book, to make others feel like they are not as weird as they think they are, and how sharing our worst moments often helps another get through their own. I asked them to comment with what peculiar habits they have. Over one hundred people commented, here are a few...

~ Amy Lyle

The proper way to eat a Snickers bar is to eat all the nougat off the bottom first and then strip the bar of all chocolate. You are left with a gooey, yummy caramel-and-peanut sticky mess. Eat that last.

~ Heather Cadorette

When opening any bag of chips, pretzels, etc., I turn it upside down and open the bottom. The seasoning/salt then drifts back down to coat the others. My children started doing this when they were very young. I am proud.

~ Alyssa Catenacci Stepp

I eat cake batter like pudding. I watch the same TV show to fall asleep every night. The proper way to eat a Kit Kat is to nibble all the edges and then eat the layers individually.

~ Meghan

I have to say goodbye to each pet and tell them when I will be back, and also which one is in charge while I'm away.

~ S.G.

My voice, speech pattern, and vocabulary change, depending on whom I am talking to. I will mirror a Michigan accent to a southern Kentucky drawl. My mom always said she could tell who I was talking to based on how I sounded.

~ Jaime Greathouse

I don't step on grates, meter covers, or any other kind of non-solid surface in the ground.

~ Brittany Evans

When I eat Ben & Jerry's Karamel Sutra with the caramel core, I always eat the ice cream around the core so that the last few bites can have gobs of gooey caramel in them.

~ S.G.

Before I can leave a hotel room, I must tidy up first.

~ Mia Moore

I sort M&Ms in ROYGBIV order and eat them first by frequency until they're even, and then one of each color in order until they're gone.

~ Christine T.

I fast-forward through my favorite dozen movies to only watch my favorite scenes.

~ Anita

I shake my towels out before I use them to check for spiders.
    ~ Karen Knight

If I have to use the bathroom in the middle of the night, I always flip the light on and off quickly to make sure there are not any creatures in the toilet.
    ~ Becky Robinson

When I am setting a timer or alarm, instead of setting it for 4:00, for example, I'll put in 3:52 or 3:47 or something like that. I like to think it saves wear and tear on the zero button, but also, I think some of those higher number buttons might feel sad they don't get used.
    ~ Sarah M

I can't wear regular T-shirts because I don't like them touching my neck. I don't wear lipstick because I hate the feeling of stuff on my lips.
    ~ Meghan

When I give my patients a cup with a straw to take meds, I find myself making the sucking face along with them.
    ~ Jessica Byrne

I use a Kleenex more than once before throwing it away. I start in one corner, then move to an unused part for the next use. I can usually get about three or four nose blows out of it before it's done.
    ~ Sarah M

If anything requires a code or fingerprint scan, I have to wipe it first. I carry a pack of sanitizing towelettes and I use them on ATM machines, the gym entrance scanner, my apartment gate code, and even the numbers on the microwave at work.

~ Tina M.

I buy only three bananas - no more, no less.

~ Elaine Garcia

I peel dead skin and calluses from my heels when I'm watching television.

~ Amanda Lucha

I keep a separate bottle of toothbrush-dipping Listerine to dip my brush in before I put toothpaste on it.

~ Michele Robinson

I go to sleep with my left big toe wrapped around my Achilles tendon on my right leg. I can't sleep if the blankets are covering my feet. God forbid they should be tucked in.

~ Elizabeth C.

When I'm stressed, I pluck out all my eyelashes.

~ M.W.

THE END

THANK YOU.
MERCI.
GRACIAS.

To all who inspired the stories:

- BP Pals, KKMF
- The Cumming Writer's Club
- Content editors - Becky Robinson, Michelle Franks, and Sharon Specker
- Proofreaders - Julie Carter and Ansley Millwood
- Photographs and cover design - Andrea Ferenchik
- Bio photograph - MNJ Photo
- Bio photo dress - Tory Burch via TJ Maxx
- Bio photo Hair - Sheri Ferraro at Aveda, and Diane, my neighbor
- Book editor, graphics, advice-giver, t-shirt designer and alpaca-modeling advisor - Tony Darnell
- Very-good idea provider - Becky Robinson @chattRhouse
- Alpaca voice-over artist on social media - Chris Corso
- Recipe - @momlovesbaking
- Alpaca wrangler, Sophie, from Atlanta Animal Casting
- Browns Bridge Church and my wonderful small group - *Galatians 6:2* Help carry each other's burdens…
- My family and friends for your love and support

I love you!

"AMY LOOKS A LOT OLDER IN PERSON BUT SHE MADE ME PHOTOSHOP HER"

- Andrea, photographer

"AMY IS A HIGH-FUNCTIONING DYSFUNCTIONAL"

-Her therapist

"THIS IS THE BEST BOOK YOU'LL EVER READ"

- Amy's Mom

"I KNOW AMY PERSONALLY AND SHE DOES FALL DOWN A LOT"

- Shannon

"YOU WILL FEEL 20-32% BETTER ABOUT YOUR OWN LIFE AFTER READING THIS BOOK"

- Amy's neighbor

Excerpt from *The Amy Binegar-Kimmes-Lyle Book of Failures*

A LITTLE BIT ABOUT ME

I've been married twenty years, not to the same people, but twenty years nonetheless. I understand that a successful marriage requires being a good listener, showing sensitivity toward others' needs and wants, and practicing unconditional love. I really struggle with being a good listener, showing sensitivity toward others' needs and wants, and unconditional love. I do, however, offer loyalty and humor and I am a real wildcat in the bedroom.

Everyone tells you to marry your best friend, but I take exception to this advice and have the divorce papers to prove it. Your best friend knows who's on the list of people you wish you could stab in the face; knows all your aches and ailments; is the one that helps you try to narrow down whether you have diverticulitis, irritable bowel syndrome, or a tumor in your digestive tract—things you tell your best friend, not the person you're having sex with.

Before we got married, my second husband, Peter, asked me if I was certain I could handle four children. "Sure!" I answered confidently. I was a corporate trainer for one of the biggest staffing firms in the world and thought, *"They're just kids. How difficult could it be?"*

In hindsight, I gravely miscalculated the prospect. I imagine it's like Katie Holmes agreeing to marry Tom

Cruise. She presumably thought, "so he believes in a Galactic Confederacy where people arrived on a DC-8-like spacecraft seventy-five million years ago … he's adorable!"

Sometimes you just get swept away in the moment and think you can handle anything. It was only AFTER Peter and I got married that I realized that four kids are way too many kids.

I knew I could succumb to defeat or keep trying. I opted for the latter and now live by the motto: I am not a failure. … I'm just having a little bit of trouble right now.

~ Amy Lyle

Amy Lyle lives in North Georgia with her second husband, Peter, and their four teenagers, Savannah, Madison, PJ, and Anna - plus two large dogs, Cooper and Mason.

Amy is a playwright for a large non-profit, a contributor to *My Forsyth Magazine* and is a frequent guest of WXIA's *Atlanta and Company*. Her screenplay, #fakemom will begin shooting in the fall of 2019.

To connect with Amy:
Website: AmyLyle.com
Facebook: facebook.com/amylyle.me
Twitter: @amylyle
Instagram: @authoramylyle

Buy your
"WE'RE ALL A MESS, IT'S OK"
t-shirt, sweatshirt or hoodie on Amazon.com.

Or visit: AmyLyle.com/t-shirts

WE'RE ALL A MESS, IT'S OK

Printed in Great Britain
by Amazon